HELPING TEENS
REACH THEIR DREAMS

Susanna Palomares

Dianne Schilling

Innerchoice Publishing, Spring Valley, California

Cover design: Doug Armstrong Graphic Design
Illustrations: Dianne Schilling

ISBN: 1-56499-013-3

INNERCHOICE PUBLISHING
P.O. BOX 2476
SPRING VALLEY, CALIFORNIA 91979
(619) 698-2437

The future belongs to those who believe in their dreams.

—*Eleanor Roosevelt*

Contents

Introduction

The Air Is Thick with Dreams

Young people are dreamers. The future belongs to them and they know it. They are the inventors of countless random visions of the future — exhilarating, frightening flashes of the possible and the preposterous.

Teenagers dream of being beautiful, handsome, strong, successful, rich, and in love. They dream of leaving home, having a car, clothes, a house, travel, a mate, and children. They envision earning a degree, mastering a trade, being admired, desired, and respected. They feel excited about the opportunities, confused by the choices, fearful of the unknown, uncertain about the future, and, if life thus far has been bearable, cautiously optimistic about what lies ahead.

Waiting among the dreams are potential goals. Real, possible futures that need only be taken seriously for a few minutes to determine if they pass a friendly reality check and are worth pursuing. But how many of us take the time to invite teenagers to look seriously at their dreams? Which of us has come to school equipped with a reality measurement and devoted an hour to "dream examination."

Without realizing it, counselors and teachers often play the role of *dream-makers*. We say things like, "You can go to college and become an engineer," or "If I had talent like yours, I'd study acting in a minute," or "Don't waste your time here. Go to New York and become a designer." Flash — a dream is born. Each new dream takes its place among all the other dreams competing for a few seconds of conscious attention between classes, meals, homework, chores, sports, hobbies, and friends.

There's something irresponsible about adding to a teenager's dream stockpile without at least taking the time to enter the dream on an inventory list. What is the name of this dream? How much does it weigh? Does it go in the 5- or 10-year column? Is it strictly for entertainment or will it build a future?

Welcome to *Helping Teens Reach Their Dreams*.

This book will help you — a *dream-maker* — become one of the extraordinarily few adults who invites teenagers to pluck a sampling of dreams from the stockpile and examine them. One of those rare individuals who shows young people how to select viable dreams and transform them into goals, which is to say, *make them come true!*

More Than a Checklist

As long as dreams are floaters "out there," they remain merely fantasies, accessible to the conscious mind but having little real impact on the brain. To reach their dreams, teenagers have to mix a little mass with the ether.

The activities in *Helping Teens Reach Their Dreams* are designed to help students infuse their dreams with enough weight to bring them down to earth where they can be observed, examined, and discussed. Those that look promising become goals. Those that don't . . . well, cut them loose to float again. Perhaps they'll look better another day.

The activities are divided into six units. Three of them — **Attitude, Communication,** and **Self-Esteem** — have to do with conditions and skills that lay a strong foundation for reaching dreams or anything else. **Goal Setting** follows, and is the longest, most involved unit because this is where the transformation takes place. The final two units, **Decision Making** and **Motivation** prepare students to deal with two of the most common questions asked by people in the process of pursuing goals: "What do I do next?" and "What's the use, anyway?"

By the time students have participated in activities from all six units, they will have acquired a priceless set of tools to carry with them for the rest of their lives and open up whenever a dream floats by that looks like it might be worth examining. In addition, students will have commenced developing essential skills enabling them to effectively use those tools. Obviously, the more they practice, the more skillful they become.

How to Use the Activities

The activities within each unit are arranged in a logical order; however, feel free to pick and choose in response to the specific needs of your students. Only in the **Goal Setting** unit is it *highly recommended* that you honor the existing sequence of activities. Students are intensely involved in formulating goals at this point, and each activity adds a new and important layer to the process.

Many activities are accompanied by a "Student Experience Sheet." Experience sheets are handouts for you to duplicate and give to your students. The parent activity will tell you exactly how the experience sheet is to be used, when to distribute it, what instructions to give, etc. Experience sheets are like guided journal pages; they are highly personal and must never be collected, evaluated, or graded. Frequently, activity directions suggest that students share portions of what they have recorded (on their experience sheet) with a partner or members of a small group. Always emphasize that sharing is voluntary and that the students need not reveal any piece of information that they prefer to keep private.

At the conclusion of most activities, you will encounter a list of "Discussion Questions." Discussion questions are provided to help you involve students in a process of thinking about and summarizing the learnings derived from a particular activity. Many of the activities in *Helping Teens Reach Their Dreams* require active forms of participation — role playing, simulation, guided imagery, creative writing, etc. By bringing students together at the conclusion of the activity and giving them a few minutes to talk about the experience, you encourage cognition, the exercise of higher-level thinking skills, and the internalization of knowledge and skills.

In Conclusion . . .

If neglected, goals quickly waste away and return to the ether. Keep that in mind. Frequently remind students of their goals. Become the "Goal Person" at your school. Dangle the word off of participles. Sing it like an anthem. Wear it like a piece of jewelry.

Goals are magical. They deliver us our dreams.

Attitude

It has been said that life is forty percent what we make it, and sixty percent how we take it. Whatever the ratio, the point is clear that attitude is a defining lens. We always have a choice about how we respond to events in our lives.

To recognize the benefits of developing positive, responsible attitudes, young people must first grow in self-awareness. They must learn to understand feelings and their relationship to thoughts, and they must understand that their own feelings are normal, predictable, and susceptible to control. Feelings convey messages about conditions and events going on in the environment, and provide important clues to the way the brain is processing information. A second major dimension of attitude is self-talk. Self-talk is a category of thought that not only shapes self-concept, but predisposes individuals to succeed or fail.

Activities in this unit concentrate on developing self-awareness, and provide young people with opportunities to develop positive attitudes through constructive habits of self-control and self-talk.

Thoughts, Feelings, and Behaviors

Experience Sheet and Discussion

Objectives:
The students will:
—differentiate between thoughts, feelings, and behaviors.
—state that negative feelings are triggered by negative thoughts.

Materials:
index cards labeled with thought, feeling, or behavior words; one copy of the experience sheet, "Make Your Feelings Work for You," for each student

Directions:
Distribute two or three index cards to each student. Prepare these cards in advance by labeling them with various thought, feeling, and behavior words, as shown:

Talk about the differences between thoughts, feelings, and behaviors. Give a few examples and ask the group as a whole

Thoughts	
remembering	reasoning
thinking	questioning
figuring	concentrating
forgetting	calculating
pondering	projecting

Feelings	
joy	delight
anger	worry
fear	loneliness
depression	apathy
surprise	curiosity

Behaviors	
running	kissing
talking	discussing
dancing	studying
playing	arguing
watching TV	working

to name the category to which each belongs. Then have the students take turns reading their cards aloud, identifying the appropriate category. Continue until the students appear to have grasped the concept.

Distribute the experience sheets. Give the students about 15 minutes to complete the sheet. Then ask them to form small groups and share what they have written. Conclude the activity with a class discussion.

Discussion Questions:

1. How do thoughts affect feelings? How do feelings affect behavior?
2. When you have feelings that you can't explain, does that mean that they have nothing to do with your thoughts? Explain.
3. How can we control our feelings? ...our thoughts?
4. When you have feelings that you think might be affecting your health, what can you do about them?
5. Can other people ever *make* you feel a certain way? Why or why not?

Make Your Feelings Work for You!

Experience Sheet

Our feelings help us function in many ways. For example, have you ever become frightened and, because of your fear, done something to protect yourself from a real danger? If so, your feelings caused you to take positive action.

Below is a list of feeling words. Pick one or two of them, and see if you can briefly explain how that emotion affects your behavior. How does it work for you?

anger	joy	power	patience
eagerness	indecisiveness	satisfaction	love
fatigue	protectiveness	pain	hope
courage	silliness	curiosity	

_____

_____

Now think about the emotions of self-pity, greed, jealousy, and possessiveness. **How do they affect behavior? What kinds of problems can they cause?**

_____

_____

Feelings have an effect on your body. They can wound and they can heal. Feelings can get "locked in" to your body when you refuse to accept and deal with them. This is a type of stress, and when it happens, real sickness can result. **Do you remember a time when you or someone else got sick under pressure? How about a stomachache or headache just before a test?**

Sometimes feelings show in the form of a twitch or tic in a muscle; other times as a tight jaw or lost voice. **Below is a list of body reactions. Next to each one, list feelings that you think can lead to these body reactions.**

Tears _____   Smile _____

Lump in throat _____   Pounding heart _____

Sweaty palms _____   Clenched fists _____

Shaky arms and legs _____   Bouncy walk _____

Red face _____   Tight stomach _____

Frown _____   Trembling jaw _____

Squeaky voice_____   Slouched posture _____

Here are some things to try:

Get rid of old guilt feelings you may still have about something you did. The best way might be to go to the person or people you wronged, admit it, and apologize. If that isn't possible, imagine the situation. Replay it in your mind, doing what you wish you had done the first time.

Affirm yourself. People tend to like people who like themselves. You might feel ridiculous doing this, but give it a try anyway. Look in the mirror and say the nicest things you can think of to yourself *in a sincere way*. Establish a relationship with yourself as your very best friend, the person you can always count on to be on *your* side.

I Think, Therefore I Feel

Experience Sheet and Discussion

Objectives:

The students will:
— describe the causal relationship between thoughts and feelings.
— state that their feelings in a situation can be improved by changing their thoughts about the situation.
— identify personal characteristics/traits that can and cannot be changed.

Materials:

one copy of the experience sheet, "You *Can* Help How You Feel!" for each student

Directions:

On chalkboard or chart paper, make three columns. Over the first column, write the heading, "**Situation**." Over the second, write the heading, "**Thoughts**" and over the third, write the heading, "**Feelings**."

Begin by asking the students to help you generate a list of situations that typically lead to negative feelings. Responses might include:

• Not having a date for a big dance.
• Not knowing the answer when the teacher calls on me.
• Doing poorly on a test for which I studied hard.
• Eating lunch alone.
• Not being invited to a friend's party.
• Being eliminated during tryouts for a team, musical group, cheerleading squad, school play, etc.

List the situations in the first column. Then take one situation at a time, and ask the students what *thoughts* a person might be likely to have in that situation. For example, a student who has no date for an important dance might think, "I'm not fun (popular, attractive) enough." A student who doesn't know the answer to a teacher's question might think, "I always end up looking stupid." Write all suggestions in the second column.

Then ask the students how they would *feel* in each situation if they had the thoughts described. For example, a person without a date who thinks she isn't any fun might feel humiliated or depressed. The person who thinks he looks stupid because he can't answer a question might feel embarrassed or frustrated. Continue making connections between the thoughts and subsequent feelings in each situation.

Suggest to the students that the feelings in each situation can be improved by changing the thoughts from negative to neutral or positive. For example, what would happen to the feelings of the student who couldn't answer his teacher's question if he thought, "I don't know the answer, but I'll listen and find out what the answer is so I'll know it next time." Make the point that situations don't cause feelings, *thoughts* cause feelings. No one forces a person to feel a certain way in a particular situation. Suggest this idea: *The easiest way to change your feelings about a situation is to change your thoughts about it.*

Explain that using this technique can be especially helpful when dealing with physical characteristics that are out of one's control. For example, say: *If it really bothers you that you are so tall, there's not much you can do to become shorter, but you could stop telling yourself that being tall is a curse and try focusing on your positive qualities instead.*

Distribute the experience sheets. Give the students a few minutes to write down their ideas under each example. Then have them form small groups, discuss their responses, and collectively generate additional ideas. Lead a follow-up discussion.

Discussion Questions:
1. How do thoughts trigger feelings?
2. Why is it easier to change your thoughts about a situation than it is to change your feelings?
3. Why do we waste our time feeling miserable about things that we cannot change?
4. Who is in control of your thoughts?

You *Can* Help How You Feel!
Student Experience Sheet

You probably have things about yourself that you wish you could change. Some of those traits or characteristics *can* be changed—and some *can't*. But even if a trait cannot be changed, you don't have to feel miserable or depressed about it. Remember, negative feelings are caused by negative thoughts. The easiest way to stop feeling bad about a trait or characteristic is to change your thoughts about it.

So, instead of feeling embarrassed, self-conscious, or depressed about a trait, choose to do one of two things:

       1. Change (or minimize) the trait.
       2. Change your thoughts about the trait.

What could you do in each of these situations. Write down your ideas:

1. You dislike the color of your hair and think it makes you look drab.

_____

2. You are very short, and think that short people have to fight for attention and respect.

_____

3. The medication you are taking makes your face round and full. You think you look fat and ugly.

_____

4. You are self-conscious about your weight (too fat or too thin). _____

_____

5. You think you are awkward and uncoordinated. _____

_____

6. You hate your nose. _____

_____

7. You use a wheelchair and think everyone feels sorry for you, which causes you to feel resentful.

_____

8. You think your feet are too big. _____

_____

9. You have a speech impediment and think it's not worth it to try to communicate with people.

_____

10. You are self-conscious about your freckles. _____

_____

11. Other: _____

_____

_____

Can You Hear Yourself Talk?

Experience Sheet and Discussion

Objectives:
The students will:
—define positive and negative self-talk.
—identify which style of self-talk they
   predominantly use.

Materials:
one copy of the experience sheet, "When
You Talk to Yourself, What Do You Say?"
for each student

Directions:
Write the term *self-talk* on the board and
ask the students what it means to them.
Facilitate discussion, making sure to cover
the following points:

• Self-talk consists of the words you say
about *you*, either silently to yourself or
audibly to another person.

• Everything you say about yourself
(your self-talk) enters your subconscious
mind.

• The subconscious mind believes anything you tell it, whether true or false. It
makes no moral judgements; like a computer, the subconscious accepts and acts
on whatever input you give it. Whatever
you put in, you get back.

• When you say things about yourself
that are negative, you are directing your
subconscious to make you behave like a
person with those same negative qualities. When you say positive things about
yourself, you are directing your subconscious to make you behave in positive
ways.

• Self-talk is closely related to personal
effectiveness. Positive self-talk adds to
your personal effectiveness. Negative

self-talk robs you of effectiveness. The more positive the self-talk you use, the greater your personal power, and the more control you have over your life.

Write the headings, "Positive Self-Talk" and "Negative Self-Talk" on the board. Ask the students to help you brainstorm a list of statements to write under each heading. Include statements that the students can recall making as well as statements they have heard others make. (Most likely the negative self-talk list will be longer.) Leave these lists on the board, while you have the students complete the self-assessment, "When You Talk to Yourself, What Do You Say?" When they have finished, lead a follow-up discussion.

Discussion Questions:

1. What did you learn about yourself from the self-assessment?
2. Why do you think our list of negative self-talk statements is longer than the list of positive statements?
3. How does our culture encourage negative self-talk? How does it encourage positive self-talk?
4. Why is it important to know what effect your self-talk can have on your well being?
5. What specifically can you do to remind yourself to use positive self-talk?

When You Talk to Yourself, What Do You Say?

Self-Assessment

Which kind of self-talk do you engage in more, positive or negative? Take this quiz and find out. **Circle the answer that sounds most like the way you talk to yourself.**

1. You enter a swimming competition. You do your best, but you don't win. What do you say to yourself?

    a. *If I had only tried harder, I'd have done better.*

    b. *I did the best I could and next time I'll do better.*

2. You run for student body president, but don't win. What do you say?

    a. *I'm a loser; I never get chosen for anything.*

    b. *I did the best I could and next time I'll do even better.*

3. You have a day where everything just seems to go wrong. You tell yourself:

    a. *I really messed up everything today.*

    b. *Everybody has days like this sometimes, and I'm just not going to let it get me down.*

4. You put off doing a task you don't like until the last minute and now you're faced with a deadline. Which do you say?

    a. *I'm so lazy. I never do anything until the last minute.*

    b. *I'm getting better about not leaving things until the last minute. The next time I do this I'll have more time.*

5. You are about to take a test in your most difficult subject. What do you say?

    a. *I'm really dumb in this subject; I'm never going to pass this test.*

    b. *I've really studied for this test. I'm confident that I'll do well.*

Try this:

• For the next 3 days, pay close attention to your self-talk. Keep track of how frequently you use negative and positive self-talk.

• Make a conscious effort to use positive self-talk.

• Pay attention to the self-talk of the people around you.

• Tell others how they can use positive self-talk.

Talking to Yourself
Presentation, Discussion, and Experiment

Objectives:
The students will:
—recognize characteristics of high self-esteem and low self-esteem.
—learn and practice methods of positive self-talk.
—demonstrate understanding of how positive self-talk enhances self-esteem.

Materials:
chalkboard and chalk or chart paper and markers

Directions:
Ask the students if they know what is meant by the terms *self-image* and *self-esteem*. Involve the students in a discussion, making these points about the importance of self-esteem and the role of self-talk in building high self-esteem.

• **Self-image is the picture you have of yourself.** Self-esteem is how you *feel* about that picture. If you like the picture (the total person, not a photograph or image in the mirror); if it makes you feel strong, powerful, and capable, then you probably have high self-esteem. If you *don't* like the picture, if if makes you feel inferior, powerless, and incapable of doing things well, then you may have low self-esteem. Of course, your self-esteem can be anywhere in between, too.

• **Your self-esteem significantly impacts how you behave, learn, relate, work, and play.** With high self-esteem, you are poised and confident, have generally good social relationships, are less influenced by peers, and usually make good decisions. With low self-esteem, the reverse is generally true.

• **Self-esteem, whether high or low, tends to be self-perpetuating.** When you feel good about yourself, you project confidence and people treat you differently than they do when you feel poorly about yourself. Because you are treated well, your positive beliefs about yourself are reinforced and validated and you project even greater confidence, thus perpetuating a positive cycle. Conversely, a negative cycle occurs when you expect and project negative things about yourself. Over time, if you have high self-esteem, you:

—are proud of your accomplishments.

—tolerate frustrations as they come along.

—take responsibility for your actions.

—approach new challenges with enthusiasm.

—experience a broad range of emotions and feelings.

If you have low self-esteem, you:

—avoid situations and experiences that involve risk.

—down play or belittle your talents as not being good enough.

—blame others for your failings.

—are easily influenced by others.

—feel powerless, and are frequently defensive.

—are easily frustrated.

• **Disappointments happen on a daily basis and can affect you for better or worse, depending on how you *react* to them.** How you react is frequently based on how you feel about yourself. When you fail a test in school, if you have high self-esteem, you look at your own responsibility in the failure. You might think you could have studied more, or that next time you will pass, or that it is simply a tough subject for you. If you have low self-esteem and fail a test, you are more likely to blame the teacher or the system and to conclude that you're incapable. Your low self-esteem causes you to draw a false conclusion and verbalize it to yourself by thinking, "I must be stupid," instead of "I feel bad about failing, but it's not the worst thing that could happen. I'll do better next time." Such verbalizations are examples of **SELF-TALK**.

• **When you were very young, one of the main ways you developed self-esteem was by paying attention to how your family, teachers, and friends treated you, and how they talked about you.** If they liked you and said you were a worthwhile person, then you had good reason to feel the same way about yourself. Today, what others think and say about you is still important, but even more important is what you think about yourself, and what *you say to yourself*. Now that you're not a child anymore, the most powerful influence on your self-esteem is your own self-talk.

• **Be watchful of your self-talk.** The more positive your self-talk, the higher your self-esteem, the more negative your self-talk, the lower your self-esteem. If you find yourself saying something negative or seeing the worst possible side of a situation, tell yourself, "Stop!" Discontinue the negative thought and substitute a positive thought.

Describe situations that could lead to negative self-talk. Have volunteers give an example of negative self-talk followed by an example of positive self-talk for each situation:

1. You strike out in a ball game.
2. You find out your parents are divorcing.
3. You get a poor grade in a class.
4. You don't make the team.
5. You are eliminated in the second round of tryouts for the cheerleading squad.
6. You lose in an election for A.S.B. or class office.
7. When you and your best friend go places together, he or she always seems to get more attention from the opposite sex than you do.
8. You fall down during a jazz-dance recital.

Tell the students that for the next four weeks, you want them to work with a partner, consciously practicing the use of positive self-talk. Explain that the partners are to monitor, encourage, and assist each other.

They are to act as an extra set of ears, calling attention to negative self-talk and reminding their partner to substitute positive self-talk. Once a week, hold a 10-minute debriefing period and ask partners to evaluate their progress.

At the end of the 4 weeks, facilitate a follow-up discussion.

Discussion Questions:
1. How does self-talk affect self-esteem?
2. Why is it important to build your self-esteem?
3. Under what circumstances did you tend to use negative self-talk?
4. When did you have difficulty using positive self-talk?

Coping with Anger
Experience Sheet and Discussion

Objectives:
The students will:
—learn and practice acceptable ways to express negative emotions.
—identify feelings that typically precede/precipitate anger and discuss ways of dealing with them.

Materials:
one copy of the experience sheet, "Getting a Handle on Hostility," for each student

Directions:
Write the heading, "Anger" on the chalkboard. Ask the class to brainstorm specific examples of angry behavior and list them beneath the heading. Then read the following scenario to the class:

Laura is a bright girl and an average student. She blames her mother for her parents' recent divorce and for the fact that she rarely sees her father, whom she misses. Laura's mother works long hours and frequently doesn't get home until 7 p.m. or later. Laura's grades are dropping and she has been hanging out with some kids who use drugs. Today, Laura comes to math class unprepared. Throughout most of the class, she talks and tries to antagonize other students, which thoroughly frustrates the teacher. In addition, Laura sarcastically criticizes the previous day's homework assignment, which she found extremely difficult and failed to complete. After speaking to Laura a number of times, the teacher finally writes a referral and sends her to the office for discipline. At first Laura is surprised and tries to talk her way out of the referral. The teacher will have none of it. By the time she gets to the office, Laura is seething. She is rude to the secretary, blames the teacher for her upset, and threatens to quit school. Later that day, she finds the teacher's car and scratches the paint on one side. Then she heads for the park to meet her friends and share a joint.

Following the story, facilitate discussion by asking these questions:
—What do you think is going on with Laura?
—Why did she criticize the homework assignment?
—What were her first emotions when the teacher handed her the referral?
—Could she have expressed those emotions? If so, how? If not, why not?
—Why did Laura scratch her teacher's car?
—Why do you think Laura is using drugs?
—What actions could help Laura get control of her life before things get even worse?

Make the following points in a discussion about anger:
• Anger is a normal emotion. We all get angry and need to learn acceptable and effective ways to deal with anger.
• Anger tends to be a secondary emotion. In other words, one or more *other* feelings usually precede anger. For example, when Laura found herself facing a referral, her first emotions were surprise and shock. Next, she may have felt humiliation, panic, regret, and desperation in rapid succession. She tried unsuccessfully to defend herself. Her efforts frustrated, Laura headed for the office with anger building inside her.
• When a teenager comes home very late from a date, a worried parent erupts almost immediately in anger, but the first feeling—the unexpressed feeling—is relief. "Thank heavens, you're okay."
• When a student fails a test for which she or he studied many long hours, the first feelings are overwhelming disap-

pointment and frustration. But anger may follow so quickly it's the only emotion the rest of the class observes.
• Other people usually have difficulty coping with someone's anger. This is partly because anger acts as a mask, hiding what is really going on. Others will have a much easier time responding to your frustration, grief, relief, sadness, or fear than to your anger. Consequently, a very valuable skill to develop is the skill of expressing your initial feelings, rather than just your anger.
• Anger puts stress on the body and can lead to illness.

Distribute the experience sheet. Go over the directions and give the students a few minutes to read the three situations described. Then have the students form small groups. Direct the groups to discuss the situations and brainstorm answers to the questions, recording ideas on their individual sheets. When the groups have finished, lead a culminating class discussion.

Discussion Questions:
1. What did you decide were Mark's first emotions? ...Jennifer's? ...Sam's?
2. How could each character have expressed his or her first emotions?
3. What other alternative behaviors did you come up with in each situation?
4. How does anger mask what is really going on?
5. Why is anger such a difficult emotion to deal with in other people?
6. If you have difficulty dealing with anger, what can you do to get help?

Recommended extension:
Have volunteers role play several of the best alternatives suggested in each situation.

Getting a Handle on Hostility
Student Experience Sheet

Read the situations and see if you can empathize with Mark, Jennifer, and Sam enough to understand the emotions that *led to* their anger. Then brainstorm four alternative behaviors that would have achieved better results in each situation.

Situation 1: During a varsity baseball game, Mark ignores the base coach's signal and races for third base. As he slides into base the umpire calls him out. Mark immediately argues and makes rude remarks about the umpire's ability to see and judge the play. He continues his remarks as he moves toward the dugout. He kicks dirt, says things to the opposing team, and makes a gesture to the umpire who then kicks him out of the game. After he leaves the field, he shouts more angry remarks.

What were Mark's first feelings after he realized his mistake?

_____

How could he have expressed those feelings?

1._____ 2._____

List two other positive alternative behaviors:

3._____ 4._____

Situation 2: Jennifer works at a fast food restaurant. She does not like working the drive-thru window but is often assigned that task. Two of her responsibilities are to ask the customers if they want drinks with their order and to offer new items on the menu. Jennifer tends to ignore that part of the job because the pressure is usually so intense that she can barely get the orders filled. Her manager has spoken to her before about the necessity of following these procedures. Today, Jennifer is more harried than usual and doesn't offer the new items or ask about drinks. On her break, the manager talks to her and tells her she must improve in this area or she will be fired. Jennifer glares at the manager, tenses her body, and grumbles, "If they want it, they'll order it. I shouldn't have to ask." The manager says it is part of the job. Jennifer cries, "You're never satisfied. I can't do anything right. I quit!"

What were Jennifer's *first feelings* when her manager confronted her?

_____

How could she have expressed those feelings?

1. _____   2. _____

List two other positive alternative behaviors:

3. _____   4. _____

Situation 3: At home, Sam has been told repeatedly to clean his room. Frankly, it's become such a terrible mess that he doesn't know where to start. Besides, part of the reason it's a mess is that his older brother, who has gone off to college, is still taking up half the closet space. Today his mother has insisted that he will not go out with his friends again until his room is clean. Sam slams his bedroom door hard, takes a kick at the door leaving black scuff marks on it, and then makes a fist and punches a major hole in the wall. He lies down, lights up a cigarette, and plans how he will wait until his mother is busy and then go out to meet his friends anyway.

What were Sam's *first feelings* after his mother threatened to ground him?

_____

How could he have expressed those feelings?

1. _____   2. _____

List two other positive alternative behaviors:

3. _____   4. _____

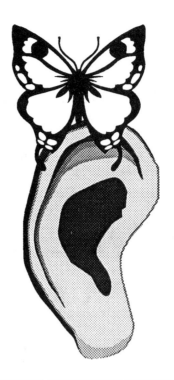

Communication

Communication skills are vital to developing and maintaining healthy relationships, and consist of effective listening, observing, speaking, and nonverbal expression. Through listening, young people gather information, develop working relationships, foster intergroup harmony, and build trust. Skillful listening is required for engaging in conversations and discussions, negotiating agreements, resolving conflicts, and many other activities of an interpersonal nature. Students use verbal and nonverbal communication to articulate ideas, ask questions, clarify directions, socialize, and plan. Effective use of language requires more than grammar and vocabulary skills. The use of "I" messages allows an individual to be assertive, while promoting understanding and preserving harmony. Observation skills include the ability to accurately interpret the nonverbal communication and body language of others.

Activities in this unit give students many opportunities to practice active listening and "I" messages, interpret nonverbal messages, and develop the ability to clearly and assertively express their thoughts, feelings, ideas, and visions.

Identifying Blocks to Communication

Role-Play and Discussion

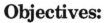

Objectives:

The students will:
—demonstrate common ways of responding to another person that may block communication.
—describe how different ways of responding may affect a speaker.
—discuss what constitutes effective and ineffective communication

Materials:

one copy of the "Communication Blockers" experience sheet for each student; chalkboard and chalk or chart paper and magic marker

Directions:

Write the following list on the board or chart paper for the students to see when they enter class:
• Interrupting
• Challenging/Accusing/Contradicting
• Dominating
• Judging
• Advising
• Interpreting
• Probing
• Criticizing/Name-calling/Put-downs

Begin the activity by asking the students to think of a heading or title for the list on the board. Write their suggestions down and discuss each one briefly. Add the suggested title, "Communication Blockers," and ask the students if they can imagine how these behaviors might have the effect of hampering communication—or blocking it altogether.

Ask the students to help you role-play each behavior to see what kind of effect it does have on communication. Invite a volunteer to start a conversation with you.

Explain that he or she may talk about anything that comes to mind, and should attempt to continue the conversation as long as possible, or until you call time.

As the student begins to speak, respond with one of the communication blockers from the list. Use appropriate gestures, volume, and tone, and make your response as convincing as possible. Continue using examples of that particular communication blocker until (1) the student gives up talking, or (2) the point has been sufficiently made.

After each demonstration, lead a class discussion about the effects of that communication behavior. Ask the discussion questions listed at the end of these directions, and others suggested by the demonstration. *The following elaboration on the communication blockers includes suggestions for conducting each demonstration, as well as important points to make during discussion.*

Interrupting
Demonstration: Butt in time and again as the student talks, with statements about yourself and things that have happened to you. For example, if the student says, "I have a friend named Sue, and...," interrupt with, "Oh, I know her—well, a little. We met the other day when...etc., etc."
Discussion: Point out how frustrating it is to be interrupted, and how futile it is to continue a conversation when interruptions occur over and over. Interrupting is probably the most common way in which communication is stopped.

Advising
Demonstration: Give lots of unasked-for advice. Use statements like, "Well, if I were you...," "I think you should...," and

"Have you tried..." If the student says, "I have a friend named Sue, and...," respond with, "Sue has a lot of problems. Take my advice and steer clear or her." or "Be careful what you tell Sue. She can't keep a secret for three minutes." Etc.
Discussion: By giving unsolicited advice, a person immediately assumes a position of superiority. Advice-giving says, "I know better than you do." Advice may also cause the speaker to feel powerless to control his or her own life.

Judging
Demonstration: Evaluate the student and everything he or she says. For example, if the student says, "I have a friend named Sue, and...," say, "Yeah, Sue's part of that stuck-up snob crowd." If the student says, "I want to see that new De Niro movie." say, "Don't waste your money, it's lousy."
Discussion: Judging retards communication even when the judgment is positive. Not only does the "judge" assume a superior position, his or her evaluations may so completely contradict the speaker's own feelings that a contest or argument ensues—or further communication seems pointless.

Interpreting
Demonstration: Analyze everything the student says in order to reveal its "deeper meaning." If the student says, "I have a friend named Sue, and...," say, "You think having Sue as a friend will improve your popularity." If the student denies the desire to be popular, say, "I think that's just a reflection of your self-image."
Discussion: Interpreting and analyzing say that the listener is unwilling to accept the speaker (or the speaker's statements) at face value. Not to mention that the interpretation is frequently wrong.

Dominating

Demonstration: Take over the conversation. If the student says, "I have a friend named Sue, and...," jump in with, "I know Sue's brother. He is..., and not only that, he..., and so..., because..., blah, blah, blah, etc., etc., ad nauseam.

Discussion: We all know how frustrating and annoying it is to be in a conversation with someone who always has something better and more interesting to say than we do. In addition, when one person dominates a conversation, others are forced to use another communication stopper, *interrupting*, just to get a word in.

Probing

Demonstration: Ask question after question in a demanding tone. If the student says, "I have a friend named Sue, and...," ask, "Why do you hang out with her?" As soon as the student begins to answer, ask, "How long have you known her?" "Is her hair naturally blonde?" And so on.

Discussion: Probing tends to put the speaker on the defensive by asking him or her to justify or explain every statement. More importantly, questions may lead the speaker away from what she or he originally wanted to say. The questioner thus controls the conversation *and* its direction.

Challenging/Accusing/Contradicting

Demonstration: Contradict what the student says and accuse him or her of being wrong. For example, if the student says, "I have a friend named Sue, and...," say, "She's not really your friend. You know her because she's Anna's friend." If the student says, "Sue and I have a lot in common." say, "You're dreaming. Name one thing!"

Discussion: Contradictions and accusations put the speaker on the spot, and make it necessary for her or him to take a defensive position. They also say to the speaker, "You are wrong." or "You are bad."

Criticizing/Name-calling/Put-downs

Demonstration: Make sarcastic, negative remarks in response to everything the student says. If the student says, "I have a friend named Sue, and...," say, "You jerk, what are you hanging out with her for." If the student says, "Because I like her..." respond, "You never did have good sense."

Discussion: Criticism diminishes the speaker. Few of us want to continue a conversation in which we are being diminished. Name-calling and put-downs are frequently veiled in humor, but may nonetheless be hurtful and damaging to a relationship.

Discussion Questions:

1. How did you (the speaker) feel?
2. What effect does this type of response have on the speaker? ...on the conversation? ...on the relationship?
3. Has this ever happened to you? What did you say and/or do?
4. Under what circumstances would it be okay to respond like this?

Communication Blockers

Student Experience Sheet

Have you ever tried to have a conversation with someone who wouldn't let you finish a sentence? Have you ever attempted to discuss a problem with someone who had an answer for everything? Bad communication habits can stop a conversation short. Here are a few to avoid:

Interrupting

Interruptions are the most common cause of stalled communication. It's frustrating to be interrupted in the middle of a sentence, and when interruptions happen over and over again, talking begins to feel like a waste of time.

Advising

Few people enjoy getting unasked-for advice. Statements that begin with, "Well, if I were you...," or "If you ask me...," are like red flags. Advice-giving says, "I'm superior. I know better than you do." Advice can also cause a person to feel powerless—as though she can't make a good decision on her own.

Judging

When you tell people that their ideas or feelings are wrong, you are saying in effect that you know more than they do. If your ideas are drastically different from theirs, they'll either defend themselves (argue) or give up on the conversation. Even positive judgments like, "You're the smartest student in class," don't work if the person you're talking to doesn't *feel* very smart.

Interpreting

Some people develop a habit of analyzing everything (including statements) to reveal "deeper meanings." When you interpret or analyze, you imply an unwillingness to accept the speaker or the speaker's statements just as they are. Analyzing is for psychiatrists and counselors, and a lot of the time even *they* are wrong!

Dominating

We all know how frustrating and annoying it is to be in a conversation with someone who always has something better and more interesting to say than we do. In addition, when you dominate a conversation, others are forced to use another communication stopper, *interrupting*, just to get a word in.

Probing

Asking a lot of questions ("Why did you go there?" "Whom did you see?" "What did he do?") tends to put the speaker on the defensive by requiring her to explain every statement. More importantly, your questions may lead the speaker *away from* what she originally wanted to say. If you ask too many questions, you are controlling, not sharing, the conversation.

Challenging/Accusing/Contradicting

There's nothing more frustrating than trying to talk with someone who challenges everything you say, insists that your ideas are wrong, or states that what happened was your fault. Contradictions and accusations put the speaker on the spot, and make the speaker defensive.

Criticizing/Name-calling/Put-downs

Don't make sarcastic or negative remarks in response to the things someone says. Criticism whittles away at self-esteem. Hardly anyone wants to continue a conversation that's making him feel bad or small. Even name-calling and put-downs that sound funny can still be hurtful. In the long run, they damage friendships.

Play It Back!
Dyad Sequence and Discussion

Objectives:
The students will:
—demonstrate attentive listening with a series of partners.
—state how they let others know they are listening.

Materials:
chalkboard and chalk

Directions:
Assign the students to groups of eight or ten. (An even number in each group is essential for this activity to work. If a group is one short, join that group during the activity.)

Ask the students to choose a partner. Explain that both people will take turns speaking to the same topic. As the first person (**A**) speaks for 1 minute, the second person (**B**) must listen very carefully, gathering information very much like a tape recorder. The listener should not interrupt or ask questions, except for clarification. When time is called, **B** will have 1 minute to "play back" to **A** as accurately as possible what he or she heard. Then **A** and **B** will switch roles. **B** will become the speaker and talk about the same topic for 1 minute while **A** listens. Then **A** will have 1 minute to "play back" what she or he heard. This will complete the first round, and the students will find new partners within their group.

Signal the end of each minute and give clear instructions. Conduct enough rounds so that every person is paired once with every other person in his or her group. (For example, if groups contain eight students, conduct seven rounds.)

Suggested topics:
"My Favorite Hobby or Pastime"
"My Favorite Food"

"My Favorite TV Show or Movie"
"My Favorite Story, Poem, Book, or
 Magazine"
"My Favorite Animal"
"My Favorite Game or Sport"
"My Favorite Song or Musical Group"
"Something That Makes Me Happy"
"Something I Want To Do This Weekend"
"Something I'm Looking Forward To"

Discussion Questions:

1. How did you feel as the speaker during this exercise?
2. How did you feel as the listener?
3. What was hardest about listening like a tape recorder?
4. Did speaking and/or listening get harder or easier as you went from partner to partner?
5. Of what value is silent, attentive listening to effective communication? Why is it a good idea to "play back" what you hear?
6. What are some things you can do to show someone that you are really listening?

The Active Listener

Communication Skill Practice

Objectives:

The students will:
—define the role of the receiver in communication.
—identify and demonstrate "active listening" behaviors.

Materials:

a diagrammatic model of the communications process drawn on the chalkboard or chart paper (see Student Experience Sheet for model); a list of topics written on the chalkboard (see below); one copy of the "Listening Actively" experience sheet for each student

Procedure:

On the chalkboard and chart paper, draw a simple diagram illustrating the communication process. For example, print the words, **SENDER** and **RECEIVER** and draw two arrows—one going in each direction—

between the two words. Explain to the students that in order for two people to enjoy and encourage each other, to work, play, or solve problems together, they need to be able to communicate effectively. In your own words, say: *In every example of communication, no matter how small, a message is sent from one person (the sender) to the other person (the receiver). The message is supposed to tell the receiver something about the feelings and/or thoughts of the sender. Because the sender cannot "give" the receiver his or her feelings and thoughts, they have to be "coded" in words. Good communicators pick words that describe their feelings and thoughts as closely as possible. Nonverbal "signals" almost always accompany the verbal message; for example, a smile, a frown, or a hand gesture. Sometimes the entire message is nonverbal. Good communicators send nonverbal signals that exactly match their feelings and thoughts.*

Ask the students to describe what a good receiver says and does to show that s/he is interested in what the sender is saying and is really listening. Write their ideas on the chalkboard. Be sure to include these behaviors:

1. Face the sender.
2. Look into the sender's eyes.
3. Be relaxed, but attentive.
4. Listen to the words and try to picture in your own mind what the sender is telling you.
5. Don't interrupt or fidget. When it is your turn to respond, don't change the subject or start telling your own story.
6. If you don't understand something, wait for the sender to pause and then ask, "What do you mean by..."
7. Try to feel what the sender is feeling (show empathy).
8. Respond in ways that let the sender know that you are listening and understand what is being said. Ways of responding might include nodding, saying "uh huh," or giving feedback that proves you are listening, for example:
    • Briefly summarize: "You're saying that you might have to quit the team in order to have time for a paper route."
    • Restate feelings: "You must be feeling pretty bad." or "You sound really happy!"

Tell the students that this type of listening is called *active listening*. Ask them if they can explain why the word *active* is used to describe it.

Ask the students to form groups of three. Tell them to decide who is **A**, who is **B**, and who is **C**. Announce that you are going to give the students an opportunity to practice active listening. Explain the process: *In the first round, A will be the sender and B will be the receiver and will use active listening. C will be the observer. C's job is to notice how well B listens, and report his/her observations at the end of the round. I will be the timekeeper. We will have three rounds, so that you can each have a turn in all three roles. When you are the sender, pick a topic from the list on the board, and remember to pause occasionally so that your partner can respond.*

Signal the start of the first round. Call time after 3 minutes. Have the observers give feedback for 1 minute. Tell the students to switch roles. Conduct two more rounds. Lead a follow-up discussion. As a reinforcement, at the conclusion of the activity, distribute the experience sheets and have the students complete them.

Discussion Questions:
1. How did it feel to "active listen?"
2. What was it like to be the observer?
3. When you were the sender, how did you feel having someone really listen to you?
4. What was easiest about active listening? What was hardest?
5. What did you learn from your observer?
6. Why is it important to learn to be a good listener?
7. How does listening help you achieve your dreams and goals?

List of topics:
"A Time I Needed Some Help"
"Something I'd Like to Do Better"
"A Problem I Need to Solve"
"A Time I Got Into an Argument"
"A Time I Had to Make a Tough Decision"
"Something I'd Like to Be or Do When I'm an Adult"

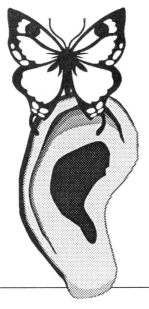

Listening Actively
Student Experience Sheet

Listening is a very important part of good communication. Listed below are characteristics of a good listener. Check the ones that describe you most of the time.

A good listener:

___ Faces the speaker.

___ Looks into the speaker's eyes.

___ Is relaxed, but attentive.

___ keeps an open mind.

___ Listens to the words and tries to picture what the speaker is saying.

___ Doesn't interrupt or fidget.

___ Waits for the sender to pause before asking clarifying questions.

___ Tries to feel what the sender is feeling (shows empathy).

___ Nods and says "uh huh," or summarizes to let the speaker know he/she is listening.

What is your strongest quality as a listener?_____

_____

_____

_____

_____

What is your weakest quality as a listener?_____

_____

_____

_____

_____

How can you become a better listener? _____

_____

_____

_____

_____

_____

```
        message
SENDER ---------> RECEIVER
       <---------
        feedback
```

When two people communicate, the process works very much like this diagram illustrates. One person (the speaker) sends a verbal message. The other person (the listener) receives that message, interprets it, and gives feedback.

The I's Have It!

Experience Sheet and Discussion

Objectives:

The students will:
—compare "I" messages and "you" messages and describe their differences.
—identify the three parts of an "I" message.
—practice formulating "I" messages.

Materials:

one copy of the experience sheet, "Don't Say 'You'—Say 'I'" for each student; chalkboard and chalk or chart paper and magic marker; diagram of the communications model (see the activity, "The Active Receiver") on the board or chart

Procedure:

Review the communications model used in the activity, "The Active Receiver." Ask the students to summarize the roles of the sender and receiver. Then in your own words, explain to the students: *When you are the sender, one of the most powerful messages you can send—especially if you are having a problem or conflict with the receiver is an "I" message. An "I" message tells the receiver what the problem is, how you feel about it, and what you want (or don't want) the receiver to do. Many times, we send "you" messages when we would be much better off sending "I" messages. "You" messages are often blaming and threatening, frequently make the receiver feel mad or hurt, usually make the problem worse, and many times don't even describe the problem. "You" messages can even <u>start</u> a conflict where none existed before.*

Extemporaneously demonstrate with one or two of your students. For example, say: *Rodney, you are fooling around again. If you don't get busy and finish that assignment, the whole group will have to stay in during the break, and it will be your fault!*

versus

Rodney, I'm worried that this assignment won't be finished by the break. I'd like to see you concentrate much harder on your work.

and . . .

Anna, are you forgetful or just lazy? Look at all those open marking pens. You ruined them!

versus

Anna, I get very discouraged when I see that the marking pens have been left open all night, because they dry out, and then we can't use them anymore. I want you to help me by remembering to cover them.

Distribute the experience sheets. Go over the directions with the students. Allow a few minutes for the students to individually complete the experience sheet.

Take one cartoon at a time, and ask two volunteers to demonstrate first the "you" message, and then their own "I" messages. Invite other members of the class to come forward, step into the role play, and substitute their own "I" message. Contrast the various efforts and discuss their effectiveness.

Discussion Questions:

1. What is the hardest part of composing an "I" message?
2. How do you feel when someone gives you a "you" message?
   ...an "I" message?
3. How can using "I" messages help us settle arguments and resolve conflicts?

Don't Say "You"—Say "I"
Student Experience Sheet

Good Communication is the Key!

When another person does something we don't like, we may be tempted to send the person a **"you" message**. "You" messages get their name from the fact that they often start with the word "you." They are blaming messages. They can make the other person feel mad or hurt—and they can make the situation worse.

Try using an **"I" message** instead. "I" messages talk about your feelings and needs. They can help the other person understand you. Here's how to make an "I" message:

1. **Describe the situation.** It may help to begin with the words, "When..." or "When you..."

2. **Say how you feel.** "When you........................, I feel............................."

3. **Describe what you want the person to do.** "When you..................., I feel..............., and I want you to......................................"

Now, you try it! Read the "you" message in the first cartoon bubble. Then write a better message—an "I" message—in the second bubble.

Words Are Only Part of It
Dramatizations and Discussion

Objectives:

The students will
—demonstrate that communication involves much more than the simple transmission of words and ideas.
—discuss how feelings are conveyed in communication.

Materials:

chalkboard and chalk; one copy of the "Body Talk" experience sheet for each student

Directions:

Prior to class, write the following words on the board:

delight	confusion
surprise	worry
hate	sadness
love	irritation
anger	fear

Begin the activity by briefly reviewing the list of words with the students. Point out that these are just some of the many emotions people feel. Explain that communication involves much more than the simple use of words. Emotions get into the act in a number of ways.

Illustrate the point by silently selecting one of the emotions listed on the board and asking the class to guess which one it is while you repeat a tongue twister. Say the tongue twister and, with your tone, inflection, facial expression, posture, and movements, simultaneously convey the emotion you selected. After the laughter subsides, allow the students to guess which emotion you were trying to convey. Then ask them how they knew. List the clues they mention on the board.

Repeat the tongue twister once or twice, conveying other emotions from the list.

Discuss with the class the specific tones, inflection, facial expressions, body postures, and movements you used to express each feeling.

Invite the students to demonstrate other emotions. Have volunteers come to the front of the class and repeat the process. Introduce a new tongue twister from time to time. After each demonstration, ask the class to examine the manner in which the emotion was communicated. Ask questions such as:

1. Can you describe the tone and inflection?
2. What did his face do?
3. What was her posture like?
4. How did she move her body?

Tongue Twisters
- Rubber baby-buggy bumpers
- She sells sea shells down by the sea shore.
- Peter Piper picked a peck of pickled peppers.
- How much wood would a woodchuck chuck if a woodchuck could chuck wood?
- Big black bugs bleed blood.

After some or all of the emotions listed have been demonstrated, vary the activity. Restrict what the performers can do. First, ask them not to move their bodies in any way, using words, tone, and inflection only. Second, ask them to convey the emotion completely nonverbally, depending only on facial expressions, posture, and body language.

Distribute the "Body Talk" experience sheets. Give the students a few minutes to fill them out. Lead a follow-up discussion.

Discussion Questions:
1. How do people communicate without words?
2. Why do you think tongue twisters were used in our dramatizations, instead of important ideas?
3. How can you hide your feelings when you are communicating with someone? What effect does that have on communication?
4. What did you learn from this activity? ...from the experience sheet?

Body Talk
Student Experience Sheet

You communicate with your body all the time. As you react emotionally to events in your life, your body takes on different postures and positions.

Think of a time recently when you experienced the following emotions. What did you do with your body? How do you think your body looked to others? Describe your body language below:

Embarrassment: _____

_____

_____

_____

Excitement: _____

_____

_____

_____

Nervousness: _____

_____

_____

_____

Boredom: _____

_____

_____

_____

Follow My Lead
Group Experiment and Discussion

Objectives:
The students will:
—use precise verbal and nonverbal communication to lead a partner to a hidden object.
—describe the importance of precise communication.
—state how effective communication contributes to personal success.

Materials:
a large open area, as free as possible of physical obstacles; scarves, large handkerchiefs, or strips of opaque fabric to use as blindfolds

Directions:
Note: You may wish to conduct the second round of this activity in a series of three to five 3-minute segments. This will limit the number of pairs on the floor at any given time, diminishing sound interference and increasing safety.

Begin the activity by talking briefly about the need for clarity, accuracy, and conciseness in communication. Announce that the students are going to participate in an activity that will test their ability to communicate with clarity.

Have the students choose partners and decide who will be the Leader in the first round. Then, in your own words, explain: *When you are the Leader, you are going to use clear, precise verbal communication to guide your partner, who will be blindfolded, to an object hidden somewhere in the room. You must use as few directions as possible, so pick your words carefully. Stay close to your partner, talking quietly by distinctly, but DO NOT touch your partner. Blindfolded partners may ask questions for clarification. Remember that other pairs will be moving about the room, and it is your responsibility as the leader to prevent collisions. At the end of 3 minutes, I'll call time and you will switch roles for the second round.*

Together, have each pair pick an object (book, key, pen, backpack, etc.) to be "found" during the activity. Instruct the Leaders to blindfold their partners. Then give the Leaders 1 minute to hide their object somewhere in the room.

Allow about 3 minutes for the Leaders to guide their partners to the hidden objects. Then gather the class together and give these instructions for the second round: *The goal of the Leader is the same in the second round—to lead your blindfolded partner to a hidden object. However, this time you must do the guiding nonverbally. You MAY NOT touch your partner, but you will have 2 minutes before the round to agree on a series of signals for various movements, such as Left, Right, Stop, Up, Down, etc. You may use claps, snaps, stomps, taps or any other clear signal that you can invent. Blindfolded partners may ask questions for clarification; however, Leaders may not answer in words.*

Have the partners pick a second object. Allow 2 minutes for signal planning. Then have the Leaders blindfold their partners and hide the object. Allow 3 minutes for the Leaders to guide their partner to the object. Conclude the activity with a class discussion.

Discussion Questions:
1. What was it like to be the Leader in round one? ...in round two?
2. How did you feel when you were the blindfolded partner?
3. How successfully did you communicate as a Leader?
4. What were some of the problems you encountered and how did you solve them?
5. What did you learn about communication from this activity?

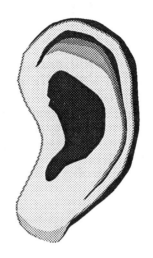

Words and Symbols
Communication Experiments and Discussion

Objectives:
The students will:
—participate in a conversation in which everyone has a vision loss.
—describe how vision and observation contribute to communication.

Materials:
scarves, handkerchiefs, or strips of opaque fabric to use as blindfolds; a list of discussion topics written on the chalkboard

Directions:
Announce that the students are going to participate in an experiment in which communication will take place with limited physical senses. Vision and the ability to observe will be lost.

Have the students sit together in groups of four. Allow the groups about 1 minute to agree on a discussion topic (from the list on the board). Then distribute the blindfolds and allow another minute or so for the students to blindfold themselves or each other.

Have the groups discuss their topic for 10 to 15 minutes. Then ask them to remove their blindfolds and, remaining in their small groups, share their reactions to the experience. Lead a follow-up class discussion.

Discussion Questions:
1. What was it like to have a conversation with everyone blindfolded?
2. What did you notice about your own listening during this experiment? What did you notice about your speaking?
3. What did being sightless demonstrate to you about the role of vision in communication?
6. What did you learn about communication from this experiment?

Suggested Conversation Topics

"Highlights of My Daily Routine"

"My Favorite Saturday (or Sunday) Afternoon"

"Something I Want to Accomplish"

"A Way I Earn Money"

"How I Help Out at Home"

"My Favorite Vacation"

"If I Could Go Anywhere, I'd..."

Giving and Receiving Feedback

Experience Sheet and Discussion

Objectives:
The students will:
—practice a process for giving and receiving constructive feedback.
—identify opportunities for giving and receiving feedback.

Note: Use this activity as an immediate follow-up to some other activity involving group participation. For best results, implement with students/groups who have worked together long enough to feel comfortable with, and trusting of, one another.

Materials:
one copy of the experience sheet, "What Is Feedback?" for each student; chalkboard or chart paper

Directions:
Write the term *feedback* on the chalkboard and ask the students to explain what it means. Jot suggestions on the board and use them to spark discussion. At some point, compare the students' ideas to this dictionary definition:
> *the return of evaluative or corrective information about an action or process*

Ask the students if they can see how the ability to give and receive feedback benefits people. Make these points and solicit other benefits from the students:
• Giving and receiving feedback is a form of sharing.
• Feedback helps us see ourselves more clearly.
• Feedback helps us to change our behaviors and those of others.
• Feedback tells us how we affect others.
• Feedback encourages honesty and builds trusting relationships.

• Feedback allows us to learn and to consider new viewpoints.

Announce that the students are going to practice giving each other feedback. Have them get together in their circle groups, or in the same groups that were used for a recent activity or project. Then, in your own words, explain: *You are going to give each other feedback about your participation in the _____ activity. Each person will have a turn being the Receiver. The Receiver always speaks first, saying what he or she likes and wishes to improve about his/her own participation. Then other members of the group take turns giving feedback to the Receiver.*

Distribute the experience sheets. Discuss the guidelines one at a time. Write the steps in the feedback process on the board. Go through them one at a time.

Steps in the Feedback Process:
1. Receiver shares how he or she feels about own participation.
    a. in general
    b. strongest point.
    c. one thing that can be improved.

2. Group members take turns briefly stating:
    a. one thing they like about the person's participation and want to see continue.
    b. one way (if any) they think the person can improve.

3. Person listens to feedback *without* attempting to explain, make excuses, or discount positive feedback. Questions for clarification are okay.

Ask a student to help you demonstrate. Model the process by giving that student feedback on something you have observed him or her doing recently. Be sure to observe the guidelines in your demonstration.

Have the students practice giving and receiving feedback in their groups. Allow sufficient time for every group member to receive feedback. Then reconvene the class and facilitate a discussion. Emphasize that feedback does not have to be formalized the way it was in this activity. Often, two or more people agree to give each other feedback privately and informally.

Discussion Questions:
1. How did you feel when you were giving feedback? ...receiving feedback?
2. What is the easiest part of giving feedback? ...the hardest part?
3. How much difficulty did you have as a Receiver accepting constructive criticism without defending or explaining yourself?
4. Was it hard to receive positive evaluations without discounting them? Why?
5. In what kinds of situations could you use the feedback process? How would it help you in those situations?

What Is Feedback?
Student Experience Sheet

Feedback helps people change and grow. Group members occasionally need to give feedback to someone in the group. Every member should also be open to receiving feedback from others.

Feedback Is...

- **Descriptive, not judgmental.**

    Describe what you see, without attaching labels to it. For example, say, "I like the fact that you rarely miss a meeting," instead of, "You're very dependable." Or say, "You interrupted me twice and John once," instead of, "You're rude."

- **Specific, not general.**

    Tie your comments to something specific that you saw. For example, instead of saying, "You never listen," try saying, "When we were making assign-ments during the meeting, I had to repeat yours three times."

- **Informing not commanding.**

    This is the same as using "I" messages. Say, "I haven't finished yet," rather than, "Stop interrupting me."

- **Aimed at behaviors that can be changed.**

    Don't use feedback to remind people of something over which they have little or no control. For example, don't tell a person with a speech impairment that he or she is hard to understand.

- **Asked for, not imposed.**

    Before giving a person feedback, ask for permission. For example, say, "I have some reactions to your presenta-tion. Would you like to hear them?"

Remember to ask for feedback, yourself. Say, "I'd like to hear from anyone who has a suggestion about how I could do a better job."

• **Well timed.**

The best time to give or get feedback is usually as soon as possible after the incident in question. But first be sure that both people want to do it.

• **Checked to ensure accuracy.**

To make sure you heard it correctly, restate any feedback given to you. When you *give* feedback, you can ask the receiver to do the same.

How to Receive Feedback

- Just listen.

- Don't explain.

- Don't make excuses.

- Don't discount compliments or other positive feedback.

- Ask questions only if you don't understand something.

- Say, "Thank you" or "I appreciate your feedback."

- Remember, you have a choice: You can accept the feedback and work on changing your behavior, or you can reject the feedback and decide not to change your behavior. However, keep your decision to yourself.

Self-Esteem

Without self-esteem, will young people dare to dream? And if they dare, will they believe in themselves and their abilities enough to make goals of their dreams and transform them into reality? Self-esteem is so central to our thoughts, feelings, and actions that it merits continuous, deliberate attention. Teenagers are old enough to grapple with the intangibility of the concept, and to begin consciously nurturing their own self-esteem.

Students with high self-esteem recognize and respect their innate worth and importance. This sense of innate worth is reinforced as students become more knowledgeable and skillful, and as their unique abilities are developed and recognized. When students practice any skill covered in this text, whether related to communication, decision making, goal setting, attitude, or motivation, their successful demonstration of that skill will strengthen their self-esteem. So celebrate each modicum of growth. Bring self-esteem out of the closet and develop it openly and joyously.

Name Art
Art Activity and Discussion

Objectives:

The students will:

—define themselves physically, emotionally, socially, and intellectually.

—artistically symbolize their strengths,
talents, and special abilities.

—practice methods of positive self-talk.

Materials:

newspaper or newsprint, soft pastels or
colored markers, and paper towels

Directions:

Distribute the materials and begin the
activity by having the students loosen up a
bit. In your own words, say: *Close your eyes.
. . Breathe deeply. . . Relax . . . When you feel
like it, begin to move your chalk on your paper
in any way you wish. . . Use squiggly or
broad, short, or long strokes. . . Get your
chalk going in a rhythm. . . Let your drawing*

*be abstract. . . Make motions that are free and
enjoyable to execute. . . We are not looking for
a masterpiece.*

Stop the students after about 10 minutes,
and have them form dyads. Direct the
partners to take about 1 minute each to
share their drawings.

Introduce the "Name Art" by saying: *You
are very closely identified with your name.
Without realizing it, people react to names—
their own and those of other people. Draw
your name on the paper. It can be any name
you are known by—your complete name, first
name, last name, or a nickname. Be as
creative as you like. Try to symbolize or
otherwise illustrate your feelings about your
name. Allow your drawing to describe you,
the person.*

After 20 minutes, ask the class to stop. In your own words, make this observation: *All the marks we make on paper, all the colors and shapes we choose, are extensions of ourselves—our thoughts and our feelings. Imagine that the drawing is you, and become the drawing's voice.*

Hold up your own drawing and demonstrate. Speaking in the first person, say (for example): *I am in layers. My underlying layer is soft and quiet, but my second layer is bright and dynamic. My third layer dances across the top and my fourth layer outlines and organizes everything. . . . I am many colors, but blue is my predominant hue.*

Have the students take turns showing their name art to their dyad partner. Direct them to follow your example and become their drawing's voice. Lead a follow-up discussion.

Discussion Questions:
1. What kinds of feelings did you experience during this activity?
2. What did you learn about yourself?
3. What was easiest about this activity? What was hardest?
4. What if instead of names, we all had numbers? Why is your name such a significant part of you?

In Search of the Perfect Person
Experiment and Discussion

Objectives:

The students will:

—state that there are no perfect people.

—identify examples of perfectionistic thinking.

—describe how perfectionism erodes self-esteem and esteem for others.

—challenge perfectionistic thinking in themselves and others.

Materials:

at least four of the following: pictures of Presidents of the United States, movie stars, baseball players, or different types of dogs or cats; collections of apples, pears, marbles, rocks, or other slightly different items of the same class or type

Directions:

Place the items chosen on a table and ask a few students at a time to come up and examine them very carefully. After the students have had a chance to study the items, ask the following questions (modified to suit the items chosen):

—*Which of the Presidents do you think was the most perfect President?*

—*Which one of the apples (pears, etc.) is the most perfect apple?*

—*Which one of the marbles (rocks, etc.) is the most perfect example of a marble?*

—*Which movie star is the most perfect of all movie stars?*

Ask the students whether they know why they are attempting to find the best example from the different groups of items. Elicit from them the fact that there are many fine examples in each group, and no one example is absolutely perfect.

Point out that since being perfect is impossible (and not much fun), it doesn't make sense for people to think that they and others have to be perfect to be liked, successful, or happy. Ask the students to share some perfectionistic ideas that might keep them from feeling good about themselves and others. For example:

• If I don't get all A's, I'm no good.
• If I'm not beautiful/handsome, no one will ever go out with me.
• If I'm clumsy, everyone will laugh at me.
• If I have a disability, I won't make friends.

Bring up the idea that students can help one another develop positive self-esteem by challenging perfectionistic ideas in the group. For example:

• "Mike, just because you have a speech disorder doesn't mean you shouldn't try out for the debate team. Look how you make us all think and laugh!"
• "Cheryl, you seemed embarrassed about telling us that your parents are divorced. It's difficult to let others know about things like that, but you're still the same person you've always been."
• "Ann, just because you're heavy doesn't mean you can't sing with a band. You have a terrific voice."

Ask whether the students are willing to challenge perfectionistic thinking in themselves and in other group members when they see it.

Discussion Questions:

1. How many perfect people have you met in your lifetime?
2. If you haven't met a perfect person, what do you think your chances are of meeting one in the future?
3. Do you think it is possible to be perfect? What would being perfect be like?
4. Do you think you were born with perfectionistic ideas, or did you learn them? If so, how did you learn them?

The First Time I. . .

Dyads and Discussion

Objectives:
The students will:
—recognize and describe their own worth and worthiness.
—define self physically, emotionally, socially, and intellectually.
—identify strengths, talents, and special abilities in self and others.
—practice methods of positive self-talk.

Materials:
the dyad topics (below) listed on the chalkboard

Directions:
Have the students form dyads and sit facing each other. Announce that the students are going to take turns talking to each other about a series of topics. In your own words, explain: *Each person will have two minutes to speak to the topic while the other person listens. The person talking should try to be as open as she or he can comfortably be. The person listening should be as good a listener as possible, focusing on the speaker rather than paying attention to other things in the room or to personal thoughts. The listener must not interrupt the speaker for any reason during this dyad sequence.*

Begin the sequence with the first topic and call time after 2 minutes. Have the students switch roles and address the same topic again. Follow the same procedure for the remaining topics.

Ask the students to stand up and mill around the room, making contact with at least four students. Tell them that each time they make contact, they are to briefly state one thing they learned from the dyad sequence.

Have the students return to their seats and lead a debriefing discussion. Ask these and other questions:

Discussion Questions:

1. How much risk is involved in doing something for the first time?
2. What determines the level of risk involved in a behavior or activity?
3. What is the relationship between risk level and your feelings of accomplishment?
4. What do we gain be recalling accomplishments in this way?

Dyad Topics:

"The First Time I. . .

. . .Got a Job"

. . .Said 'No' to Someone"

. . .Decided to Do Something I Thought Was Important"

. . .Stood Up for My Rights"

. . .Talked to a Group of People"

. . .Tried Out for a Position, Team, Club, or Group"

. . .Spoke Up for My Beliefs"

A Feeling of Accomplishment

Oral Presentations and Discussion

Objectives:

The students will:
—identify strengths, talents, and special abilities in self and others.
—practice methods of positive self-talk.
—describe how positive self-talk enhances self-esteem.

Materials:

Directions:

Introduce the activity by saying to the students: *One of the most powerful motivators for doing something is anticipating the feeling of accomplishment that we experience when the task is finished.*

Announce that you want the students to take a mental inventory of their activities and identify one that they can always depend on to give them a sense of pride and achievement. Explain that their assignment has two parts. First, they are to prepare a brief oral presentation (3 to 5 minutes) explaining the activity they take pride in. Second, they are to bring something to class on the day of their presentation that somehow illustrates or demonstrates what they are talking about. Elaborate:

Perhaps you get enjoyment out of working with computers and can bring in a piece of software you use regularly or something that you've produced using a computer. Maybe you enjoy drawing because every completed picture is a proud new creation. If so, bring a drawing for us to see. If cooking gives you feelings of accomplishment, bring in your favorite recipe, or better yet some samples. If you like science, show us an experiment you've completed, or a science book you enjoy. Your presentation doesn't have to be extensive; we're interested in whatever you tell us.

Allow a few students a day to give their presentations and show or demonstrate the item they brought. Give every presenter your undivided attention and plenty of appreciation and recognition. On the last day of the presentations, conclude the activity with a general discussion.

Discussion Questions

1. Why is it important to accomplish things?
2. What do accomplishments have to do with self-esteem?
3. What are some examples of small, everyday accomplishments?
4. How can you use self-talk to remind yourself of your accomplishments?

I Like Me

Getting More in Touch with Me

A Guided Awareness Exercise

Objectives:
The students will:
—develop greater awareness.
—experience and describe what is going on inside of them physically, emotionally, and mentally.

Materials:
none

Directions:
Tell the students that you would like to do a guided-awareness exercise with them that will help them focus on themselves and sharpen their self-awareness. Then, read the following very slowly in a relaxed, clear tone. Allow plenty of time (at least five seconds) between images. Following the exercise, facilitate a class discussion focusing on the experience.

Get comfortable in your chair and relax your body...Close your eyes and allow whatever images enter your mind to pass through...Just take a look at them...Don't do anything about them...Be aware of the position of your body...How does the chair feel against your back and underneath you?...Feel the chair supporting you...Make yourself as heavy in the chair as you can...Feel the weight of your feet on the floor...Be aware of the space around you...Feel the temperature of the air... Feel your tongue against the roof of your mouth...Be aware of the taste in your mouth...Be aware of the temperature of the air as it enters your nose...and as you exhale...Be aware of any muscle tension in your shoulders...upper body...lower body...legs...arms...Be aware of the feelings in your throat...and in your stomach.

Now be aware of your emotions...What are your feelings?...Are you sad? ...happy? ...curious? ...Or maybe you have no special feelings right now...What are you feeling?...Where do you feel emotions in your body? What is the location?...Be aware of what area in your body each feeling covers...What shape is your feeling?...Is it moving?...If so, what kind of movement is it?...What color is your feeling?...Has it changed?...What emotion are you feeling now?...Where is it exactly in your body?

Now, become aware of what you are thinking...What thoughts are coming into your head?...Just notice them...and then let them go as though they were a flowing stream...Now take a couple of minutes to notice some more of your thoughts. (Pause for about two minutes.)

Now be aware of what you are doing...Are you moving? ...twitching? ...smiling? ...frowning? ...thinking?...relaxing?...What are you doing?

Now, keeping your eyes closed, gently come back into the room and become aware of the space around you...Picture the room you are about to open your eyes in...the walls...the floor...and all the other parts of the room...Gently and slowly open your eyes and look at the room and the people in it as though you are seeing them for the first time...What comes into your awareness?

Discussion Questions:

1. What are some of the things that came into your awareness during the exercise?
2. What emotions did you feel? Where in your body were they located?
3. How do you feel now?

Success Bombardment

Experience Sheet and Group Exercise

Objectives:

The students will:
—recognize and describe their own worth and worthiness.
—identify strengths, talents, and special abilities in themselves and others.
—practice positive self-talk.

Note: For optimum impact, use this activity after your students have had time to develop as a group, e.g., have experienced several activities together.

Materials:

one copy of the experience sheet, "Success Inventory," for each student; 12 small self-adhesive labels per student; and 1 copy of the "Target" worksheet for each student

Directions:

Distribute the experience sheet. Go over the directions and answer any questions. Have the students work individually to fill out the sheets. Allow about 15 minutes. If the students appear to be having trouble thinking of accomplishments, take a couple of minutes and talk to the entire class about such examples as learning to: *walk, talk, dress, dance, play, sing, count, problem-solve, read, write, love; ride a bike, skateboard, roller-skate; ski, play softball, volleyball, soccer, basketball; cook, play an instrument, use a computer, be a friend, join an organization; earn a merit badge, award, or certificate; learn to type, baby-sit, drive a car, care for a pet; etc., etc.*

When the students have completed their sheets, ask them to form groups of four or five. Give 12 small, blank, self-adhesive labels and a "Target" worksheet to each student.

Direct the students to take turns describing their accomplishments to the other members of their group. In your own words, explain: *Tell your group why you picked those particular successes. Explain how you felt about them at the time they occurred and why they are particularly meaningful to you now. Immediately after you share, the other members of your group will each make three labels that describe positive things about you based on the successes you shared. For example, the first person's labels might say, "industrious and energetic," "musically talented," and "born to lead." Then, while you hold up your "target," that person will look directly at you, tell you what he or she has written on each label, and stick the labels on your target. The other members of your group will then take a turn "bombarding" you with their success labels in the same manner. If there are three other people in your group (total of four), you will end up with nine labels on your target. A second person in the group will then take a turn reading his or her successes and being "bombarded." Then a third person will be the target, and so on.*

Circulate and assist the groups, as needed. Although the students are expected to enjoy the exercise, make sure that they appreciate its seriousness and do not engage in any kind of teasing or put-downs. If you observe any student using the third person ("She is industrious and energetic.") when labeling a "target," stop the person and help him or her rephrase the statement in the second person. ("You are industrious and energetic.") Lead a follow-up discussion.

Discussion Questions:

1. How do you feel after doing this exercise?
2. What did you learn about yourself? ...about other members of your group?
3. How did you decide which accomplishments to include on your list?
4. Why do you suppose we spend so much time thinking about our failures and deficiencies when we have all accomplished so much?
5. Where can you put your target so that it will continue to remind you of your successes?

Success Inventory

Student Experience Sheet

Your life is a chronicle of successes, one after another, year after year. The things you've accomplished could fill a book. Look back now at the child you were and the young adult you have become. Recall some of the many things you've learned and achieved, and write the most memorable here:

• **Five skills I mastered before the age of 5 were:**

1. _____

2. _____

3. _____

4. _____

5. _____

• **Four things I accomplished between the ages of 5 and 8 were:**

1. _____

2. _____

3. _____

4. _____

• Four of my achievements between the ages of 8 and 11 were:

1. _____

2. _____

3. _____

4. _____

• Three major things I accomplished between the ages of 11 and 13 were:

1. _____

2. _____

3. _____

• Three of my successes between the ages of 13 and now are:

1. _____

2. _____

3. _____

Target Worksheet

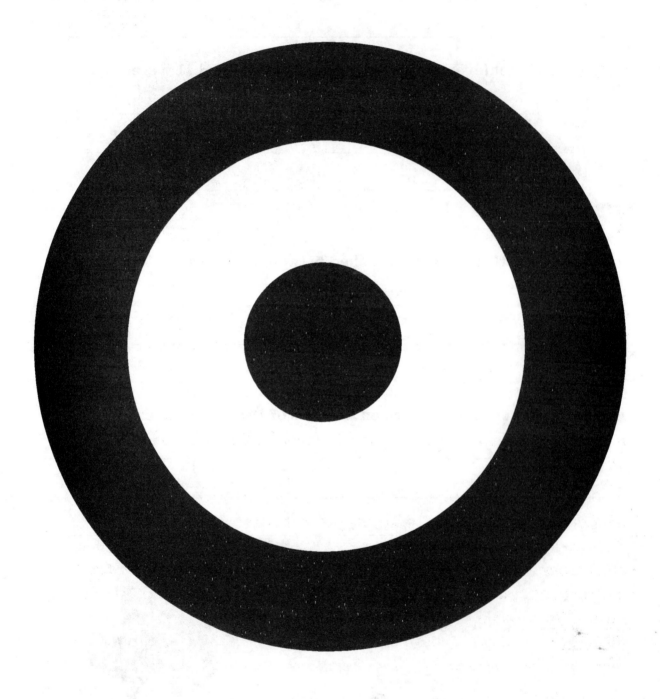

Goal Setting

Little is accomplished that isn't first the subject of a well articulated goal. The magic in goal setting is that it allows resources to come together to accomplish just about anything, and marshalling resources is a challenge that students are faced with over and over. We often think of goals in a global context, but all successful people set goals in their personal lives. Goals are stepping stones to well defined futures. They provide a sense of direction and permit decisions that advance goal attainment.

In this unit, activities enable young people to clarify their expectations, values, likes, dislikes, and dreams in preparation for setting clear, realistic goals. Students learn the importance of having an overriding vision and of aligning and attuning goals to support their vision. A goal setting process is presented in detail and students are asked to set specific, measurable goals in various areas. They learn to develop plans for accomplishing their goals, and they support those goals through the techniques of visualization and affirmation. Finally, students consider the value of rewarding themselves at each major milestone they reach.

The Power of Expectations
Discussion and Dyads

Objectives:

The students will:
—discuss the differences between their self-expectations and the expectations they have of others.
—differentiate reasonable and unreasonable expectations.
—describe how expectations shape behavior.

Materials:

chalkboard or chart paper

Directions:

Relate to the group the story of *My Fair Lady* as described in the following synopsis:

At one time, the idea that people could change themselves for the better was thought impossible. For example, if you were born poor, the expectation was that you would remain poor for the rest of your life. You could not improve or change. A writer and philosopher who believed that people could be transformed—could change and become different—was George Bernard Shaw. He said, "People are always blaming their circumstances for what they are. I don't believe in circumstances. The people who get on in this world are the people who get up and look for the circumstances they want, and if they can't find them, make them."

Shaw wrote the story Pygmalion from which the play My Fair Lady was adapted. In the play, a wealthy Englishman named Henry Higgins makes a bet with one of his friends that he can transform a young woman living in poverty on the street into a lady who will be accepted in the highest circles of society. Her name is Eliza Doolittle. Higgins has a vision of what Eliza must become in order for him to win his bet. That vision represents his expectation of her.

As the story progresses, Eliza begins to change, but very slowly. Not until she embraces Higgins' vision of her transformation can all the changes necessary for that transformation take place. Higgins' expectation must become Eliza's self-expectation.

Explain that, while it is important for others to have expectations of us and to communicate those expectations, it is far more important that *we* have quality expectations of ourselves. Make the following points about self-expectations:
- Self-expectations act as limits in every part of our lives.
- People seldom exceed their self-expectations.
- When self-expectations are low, performance is likely to be low.
- When self-expectations are high, performance is likely to be high.
- Self-expectations (as well as those of others) need to be reasonable.
- Expectations that are unreasonably high lead to disappointment.
- Expectations that are unreasonably low are limiting and also lead to disappointment.

Remind the students that when we fall short of our own expectations, we have an opportunity to examine the reasons and grow from the experience. Offer this example: *Thomas Edison invented the light bulb after hundreds of failed attempts. With each failure, Edison fell short of his self-expectation, yet learned from the experience. Years later, Edison said, "I never had any failures . . . just learning experiences." He viewed his "failures" as steps toward success.*

Reinforce the notion that whatever we're seeking to accomplish or become in life is mirrored in our self-expectations. Offer this example: *On November 3, 1992, the American people elected Bill Clinton president. Mr. Clinton had an expectation of becoming president. Only a few months before, few Americans had that same expectation of Mr. Clinton. If Clinton had listened only to the expectations of others, he'd never have won.*

After your introduction, have the students get together in dyads, and take turns speaking to the following topics, in sequence. (If necessary, the activity may be extended to a second class session.)

"When Someone Lived Up to My Expectations,"

"A Time When I Met or Exceeded My Own Expectations"

"A Time Someone Failed to Live Up to My Expectations"

"A Time I Failed to Live Up to My Own Expectations"

Discussion Questions:
1. What kinds of things can make self-expectations unreasonable?
2. How do self-expectations differ from the expectations we have of others?
3. In what ways do our expectations affect the way we behave?
4. How do you feel when someone fails to live up to your expectations? How do those feelings compare to the ones you have when you fail to live up to your own expectations?
5. How does having expectations help us achieve?
6. What happens when we have unreasonable expectations of others?

Building a Reasonable Expectation

Discussion and Experience Sheet

Objectives:

The students will:

—discuss the differences between their self-expectations and the expectations they have of others.

—describe reasonable and unreasonable expectations.

—understand how expectations shape behavior.

Note: This activity, which gives students an opportunity to consciously develop an expectation for themselves and someone else, should be completed following the activity, "The Power of Expectations."

Materials:

one copy of the experience sheet "Please, Be Reasonable!" for each student

Directions:

Remind the students that expectations can be either reasonable or unreasonable. Whether for themselves or others, reasonable expectations are more likely to be met.

Point out that one of the universal characteristics of successful people is that they have reasonable and achievable expectations of themselves and others. Suggest that to learn this skill, the students need to really think about expectations when they form them. They may need to take into account many factors in order to decide what a reasonable expectation is in a particular situation. Most people tend to form their expectations without much thought. Effective people take time to develop expectations and in so doing are seldom disappointed in themselves or others.

Have the students complete the experience sheet. Then lead a summary discussion.

Discussion Questions:

1. How do you feel about the expectations you developed?
2. How does having reasonable expectations give you greater confidence?
3. How do expectations of yourself and others differ? How are they the same?

Please, Be Reasonable!

Student Experience Sheet

We all have expectations of ourselves and others. However, most expectations are not consciously formed. In fact, if thinking is involved at all, it's usually wishful.

Here's your chance to develop four carefully thought out expectations—three for yourself and one for someone else. But before you write down each expectation, ask yourself, "What are the chances that this expectation will be met?" Think about your talents, skills, knowledge, resources, abilities, disabilities — anything that might play a role. Do the same when forming an expectation for someone else. If you see obstacles, ask yourself if they can be successfully dealt with. In short, don't write down an expectation unless you think there is a good likelihood that it will be met.

An expectation I have of myself within the next 24 hours is: _____

_____

An expectation I have of myself within the next week is: _____

_____

_____

An expectation I have of myself within the next month is: _____

_____

_____

Now, think about your friends and other people with whom you associate at school, at meetings, on teams, and at home. Choose one person and carefully form an expectation based on something specific that person is going to do.

What is the person's name?_____

What is the situation or event? _____

_____

_____

_____

What is your expectation? _____

_____

_____

_____

_____

What's So Important About Goals

Experience Sheet and Discussion

Objectives:

The students will:
—informally assess their goal-setting attitudes and behaviors.
—describe the benefits of setting and achieving goals.

Materials:

one copy of the experience sheet, "So, Who's in Charge of Your Life Anyway?" for each student

Directions:

Distribute the experience sheets. Ask the students to answer the questions at the beginning and then read the information on goal setting that follows.

Discussion questions:

1. What role do goals play in a person's life?
2. How will having goals help you?
3. Does anyone have a goal that he or she would like to share with the rest of us?
4. How do you feel after you have accomplished a goal?

So, Who's in Charge of Your Life, Anyway?

Student Experience Sheet

Without giving them a lot of thought, quickly answer these questions:

What do you want in life? _____

_____

What is one goal you have for yourself right now? _____

_____

Do you feel in charge of your life? _____

_____

Are you happy with the direction your life seems to be taking?
Why or why not?

_____

_____

Why is setting goals important? Because goals can help you do, be, and experience everything you want in life. Instead of just letting life happen to you, goals allow you to *make* your life happen.

Successful and happy people have a vision of how their life should be and they set lots of goals (both short term and long range) to help them reach their vision. A man named David Starr Jordan said, "The world stands aside to let anyone pass who knows where he is going." You can bet that those people who know where they are going are getting there by setting goals.

When you set goals, you are taking control of your life. It's like having a map to show you where you want to go. Think of it this way: You have two drivers. One driver has a destination (her goal) which is laid out for her on the map. She can drive straight there without any wasted time or wrong turns. The other driver has no goal or destination or map. He starts off at the same time from the same place as the first driver, but he drives aimlessly around, never getting anywhere, using up gas and oil. Which driver do you want to be like?

Winners in life set goals and follow through on them. Winners decide what they want in life and then get there by making plans and setting goals. Unsuccessful people just let life happen by accident. Which do you want to be? You do have a choice. Goals aren't difficult to set—and they aren't difficult to reach. You decide.

Do you remember some of the benefits of setting goals? Write down three:

1. _____

_____

2. _____

_____

3. _____

_____

Learning About Ourselves
Experience Sheet and Discussion

Objectives:
The students will:
—identify likes and dislikes and areas of strength and weakness.
—clarify personal values.
—explain how self-awareness facilitates goal setting.

Materials:
one copy of the experience sheet "Who Am I," for each student

Directions:
Pass out the experience sheets and have the students answer the questions. When they have finished, facilitate a class discussion.

Discussion Questions:
1. What have you learned about your strengths and weaknesses from this activity?
2. What have you learned about your likes and dislikes?
3. What insights did you gain concerning your values?
4. How will knowing these kinds of things about yourself help you set goals?
5. How will knowing these things help you achieve your dreams?

Who Am I?

Student Experience Sheet

An important element of successful goal setting is knowing "who you are." In order to develop goals that are meaningful, realistic, and achievable, you need an accurate sense of self-understanding. You need to know your strengths and limitations, likes and dislikes, wants and needs, beliefs and values. The following questions will help you clarify these areas:

Think back to some of the things you've learned to do in life. The following questions will get you started:

• What are five things you've learned quickly and easily? (They don't have to be school subjects.)

1. _____

2. _____

3. _____

4. _____

5. _____

• What is something that was hard to learn, that you mastered because you kept working at it?

_____

• What are some things you've been able to show other people how to do?_____

_____

• What are your major talents (strengths, abilities)? _____

_____

• What are some of your major accomplishments?_____

_____

• In what school subject or activity are you most successful?_____

_____

What about weaknesses?

First of all, everybody's got 'em. You aren't alone. Now that you've looked at some of your strengths, let's turn the coin over and look at some of the things that students say they sometimes have trouble with. If any of these apply to you, just put a ✔ next to the item:

___ 1. Using my time well
___ 2. Standing up for myself in a situation in which I know I am right
___ 3. Overcoming shyness
___ 4. Building self-confidence
___ 5. Giving myself credit for past achievements
___ 6. Giving myself credit for present strengths
___ 7. Learning from my mistakes
___ 8. Acknowledging my present weaknesses
___ 9. Starting a conversation with a member of the opposite sex

Examine yourself closely, and complete as many of the following items as you can:

My personal strengths (talents, accomplishments, favorite activities, etc.):

1. _____

2. _____

3. _____

4. _____

5. _____

My personal weaknesses (handicaps, difficulties, limitations, things I don't know how to do yet, etc.):

1. _____

2. _____

3. _____

4. _____

5. _____

If you are having trouble doing this, look more closely at what has happened to you during the past week or so.

What event or activity was a high point for you? _____

What event or activity was a low point? _____

Name one person you really enjoy being with: _____

Describe something you've experienced lately (not necessarily last week) that you hope will never happen again:

_____

Look back at what you've written. Can you spot any clues to strengths and weaknesses you haven't thought of before? If so, add them to your lists.

Now, complete the following half-sentences. Don't worry about being scrupulously honest or making perfect sense. Just have a good time looking at you.

I am a person who _____

Something I wish others could know about me is _____

One of the things I feel proud of is _____

It's hard for me to admit that _____

One of the nicest things I could say about myself right now is _____

A thing I accept in myself is _____

A thing I can't accept in others is _____

One thing that makes me angry is _____

The best thing about being a child was _____

A difficult thing about being male/female is_____

A good thing about being male/female is _____

The way I most need to improve is _____

When I feel my own energy flowing through me, I _____

When I give myself the right to enjoy life, I _____

One of the things I truly like and respect about myself is _____

I am happy when _____

I become angry when _____

I am sad when _____

I am fearful when _____

I feel lonely when _____

I have peace of mind when _____

I become frustrated when _____

I hate it when _____

I love it when _____

I get excited when _____

Admirable Qualities

List the ten qualities (such as honesty, bravery, helpfulness) you most admire in people.

1. _____

2. _____

3. _____

4. _____

5. _____

6. _____

7. _____

8. _____

9. _____

10. _____

How many of the qualities you listed do your friends have? How many do you have? What does that mean to you?

Society's Values

List ten ideals, beliefs, or values that you think all people should have. Then mark the scales below to indicate how highly you think these items are valued by society, by students at your school, and by you.

Values

1. _____

2. _____

3. _____

4. _____

5. _____

6. _____

7. _____

8. _____

9. _____

10. _____

	Low	Average	High
American Society	├───┤		
Your School	├───┤		
You	├───┤		

Stop and think about how you are expressing your values the next time you express an opinion, choose a movie or TV program, or buy something.

Developing a Personal Vision
Experience Sheets and Discussion

Objectives:
The students will:
—explain how goals give direction and purpose to life.
—state that to set meaningful goals, they must know what is important and of value in their life.
—practice describing a personal vision.

Materials:
one copy each of the experience sheets, "Man With A Vision, George Washington Carver (1864-1943)" and "My Personal Vision," for each student; writing materials; chalkboard or chart paper

Directions:
Write the heading "Personal Vision" on the board or chart paper and ask the students what the words mean to them. Accept all responses and encourage any discussion that may ensue. Record ideas under the heading.

Ask the students to turn in their workbooks to the story of George Washington Carver. Either read the story aloud while the students follow along or have the students take turns reading. At the conclusion of the story, facilitate discussion.

Discussion Questions:
1. What was George Washington Carver's vision during his young life? (to get an education) What was his vision as an adult? (to help his people and to share knowledge with them)
2. Look back through the story and identify some goals that George had at different times in his life. What was he willing to do to achieve each of these goals?
3. How were his goals tied to his vision?
4. Did an awareness of his vision help him to keep on track with his goals?
5. How did having a strong vision help him achieve his goals?

6. If George's vision had been of fame and fortune, how might his life have been different?
7. What personal characteristics did George Washington Carver have which helped him reach his goals?
8. See if you can name times in George's life when he could easily have sat back and been satisfied with his accomplishments. How did his vision keep him from doing that?

Have the students complete the experience sheet, "My Personal Vision." When they have finished writing, ask if anyone would like to share his or her personal vision with the class. Accept and validate all vision statements. Do not make (or allow students to make) any judgments. If time permits, allow the students to talk about specific things they might do to fulfill their vision (these would be their goals).

Man With A Vision

GEORGE W. CARVER (1864-1943)

George Washington Carver was born into slavery. Shortly after his birth on a farm in Missouri, his father was run over by a wagon and killed. Before George was a year old, a band of night raiders kidnapped him and his mother. His master hired a man to look for them. George was found, but not his mother.

Moses and Sue Carver kept George and gave him their name. They had no children of their own and raised George and his brother, Jim, as if they were their sons.

The Carvers were not educated people, yet they were both aware of the unusual curiosity that George had about what made things grow; he wanted to know the name of everything that grew. He made himself a secret garden where he nursed sick plants back to health. Whenever the weather permitted, George spent his Sundays in the woods. He never felt frightened or alone in the woods. He would watch the creatures moving about and study all the plant life in the woods.

Mrs. Carver taught George how to cook, clean, and sew. She got a speller for George, and he learned every word in it. He heard of a school for blacks that he wanted to attend, but it was in Neosha, eight miles away. He would have to live there. The Carvers were concerned about his survival, for he had no place to stay and no money for food; however, they knew how much learning meant to him, so they gave their consent. George was only ten years old, but he walked to Neosha with confidence. As soon as he got there, he met a black woman, Mariah Watkins, who offered him room and board in trade for work. As Mariah never had children of her own, she treated George like a son. She taught him how to wash and iron, two skills that served him well in the years to come.

The school George entered was a cabin about fourteen feet wide and sixteen feet long. He had to fight for space with the seventy-five other children who were also hungry for education. By the time George finished his chores for Mariah and did his homework, there wasn't much time for play. Sometimes he would join in the games of the other youngsters, but he was somewhat shy and not very strong for the rough and tumble games the boys liked to play.

There was no high school in Neosha. When George was thirteen, he hitchhiked a ride in a covered wagon to Kansas, where he entered high school at Fort Scott. To support himself, he worked as a houseboy for the wealthiest family in town. Again he had a home, regular meals, and a bed at night. He was very grateful for his chance at more learning.

George worked very hard at his studies. His short-term goal was to go to college, yet he knew he had to have a way to support himself. So he put to use all the skills he had learned about washing, ironing, and sewing, and he opened a laundry business!

George applied to Highland University in Kansas City. He received a letter from the University complimenting him on his fine grades and record of achievements. They said he could enroll in the fall. When he appeared for registration, the person in charge was surprised to find he was black, and would not permit George to register. He was devastated and heartbroken because he had set his heart on a college education. George began to wander across the western states, not knowing what to do.

He heard about homesteading in the desert of Kansas. George loved farming and decided to give it a try. He filed for 160 acres but had no tools to develop the claim and no money. When it was time to pay the taxes, he lost the land. He was twenty-five years old and still determined to get a college education.

Finally, George gained admittance to Simpson College in Iowa. He had only ten cents left after he had paid his entrance fees; yet somehow he was able to convince the local general store to lend him two tin tubs, a washboard, and some soap. He took in laundry and paid his way through Simpson College.

George studied art and liked to paint. He also did very well with plants and flowers. One of his teachers discouraged George from pursuing a career in art. She told him it just wasn't practical. He was told he must choose a course of study that would enable him to make a living. When his art teacher became aware of his interest in plants, she wrote her brother who was a professor of horticulture at Iowa State College. George was admitted and became the first black to graduate from that institution.

George had some difficult times at Iowa State. Black students were not allowed in the dormitory, and he was not allowed to eat in the student dining hall. But he was very determined and would not allow himself to become discouraged. He was longing to serve his people, and knew that an education would help him do it.

There were kind teachers and students at the university who wanted to help George out with gifts of clothes and money, but he would not accept them. He always insisted on working for everything he got.

George was well liked by the students, and they included him in all activities. They made him feel that the color of his skin was unimportant.

George combined his love of plants and art by painting many still-life canvases and entering them at the Iowa Exhibit of State Artists. He won several prizes, and four of his paintings were exhibited at the World's Fair at Chicago.

George enjoyed his college years. He graduated in 1894 and remained there two more years to attain his M.A. degree. He was then made an assistant instructor in botany and was placed in charge of the greenhouse. He no longer had to work as a laundryman, janitor, houseboy, or cook. George could spend all of his time on the campus and in his greenhouse. He was very happy, but he knew he must move on. He had to pursue his long range goal to help his people and to share knowledge with them.

Offers of jobs came to George from a number of Southern Negro colleges. One of the offers was from Tuskegee. Booker T. Washington, the president, wanted George to head the Department of agriculture and teach natural sciences. He accepted the position. When asked why, he said, "It has always been the one great ideal of my life to be of the greatest good to the greatest number of my people possible. I took up agriculture because I feel that it is the key that will open the door of freedom for my people. Mr. Washington feels the same way"

When he reached Tuskegee, George was given a small laboratory of his own. From this laboratory came formulas in agricultural chemistry that enriched the Southland.

Tuskegee was situated in the cotton belt. Cotton had been planted on the same acres over and over again until all the richness had been taken out of the soil. It was no longer a profitable crop. One of Tuskegee's tasks was to teach the farmers to raise other crops to save the land. George showed them the value of rotating crops. He introduced a variety of useful products derived from peanuts and sweet potatoes, two crops that grew easily in the Alabama soil.

George learned to create many by-products from peanuts and sweet potatoes. To take what one had and make it yield what one wished became his goal. Out of his experiments with the peanut came a two hundred million dollar industry.

Over the years, George W. Carver was awarded many honorary degrees. Private industry sought his services. Thomas A. Edison offered him $50,000 a year to work in his laboratories. However, George turned down each of these offers, for he cared nothing about money and never applied for a patent on any of his discoveries. He used to say, "God gave them to me. Why should I claim to own them?"

George remained at Tuskegee the rest of his life. The year 1936-37 was dedicated to him for his forty years of service to Tuskegee and the South. His fibers, paints, stains, and peanut and sweet potato products were on exhibit. There were 118 sweet potato products. Thirty-six of his paintings were displayed along with hundreds of his lace designs. There were wall paper designs and wall board, mats and rugs, and vases made from Alabama clays.

George rose from slavery to become a famous scientist, overcoming all obstacles, including those of racial discrimination.

(From *Smile, You're Worth It!*, by Margo Kluth and Dorothy McCarthy. Me and My Innerself, San Clemente, California, 1983.)

My Personal Vision

Student Experience Sheet

THE GREATEST THING IN THE WORLD IS NOT SO MUCH WHERE WE ARE....BUT IN WHAT DIRECTION WE ARE MOVING.

Think about the questions you answered in the experience sheet "Who Am I" and about what you have just learned about the power of personal vision from the story of George Washington Carver. Now put all of your learnings and reactions together, and develop some ideas about *your* personal vision. Remember, you are a unique individual and your vision and goals may be quite different from anyone else's. It's up to you to find out what your ideals and visions really are. You are the one who must decide what to pursue and in what direction to aim your goals.

Three areas I am interested in are:

1. _____

2. _____

3. _____

Three important values I hold are:

1. _____

2. _____

3. _____

A personal vision I have for my life is: _____

_____

_____

_____

_____

_____

_____

_____

_____

_____

_____

_____

_____

_____

Setting and Attaining Goals

Discussion and Experience Sheet

Objectives:
The students will:
—explain that having a goal is the first step to achieving what one wants.
—identify specific steps for attaining goals.
—develop skills in setting practical and achievable goals.
—experience goal attainment.

Materials:
pens or pencils, blank note paper, and one copy each of the experience sheets, "You Can Reach Your Goals!" and "Tips for Setting Goals," for each student

Directions:
This is a continuing activity, designed to be used with students over several weeks. It will allow them to experience the satisfaction of setting and achieving goals that are important to them, and will teach them an effective goal-setting process.

Introduce the activity. Explain to the students that most successful people have a habit of setting clear goals concerning things that they want to accomplish. Explain that in this activity, the students will set goals and experience the feeling of success that comes with attaining them.

Point out that when we think of goals, we usually picture big, important things like cars, houses, vacations, etc., but that we set dozens of smaller goals each day. Ask volunteers to share some of the things they want to accomplish today. Point out that stating these things is the simplest form of goal setting.

Distribute the experience sheets, "You Can Reach Your Goals!" and "Tips for Setting Goals." Review PART 1 of the goal-setting experience sheet, offering an example or two to illustrate each point. Then give the students a few minutes to complete the first part of the sheet, writing down their goals and answering the questions.

If possible, spend a few moments with each student, reviewing his or her goals to make sure that they are attainable, properly written, and within the purview of the student to achieve (not dependent on events or people outside the student's control).

Explain that goals are achieved in steps. Success is measured as each step is completed. Point out that PART 2 of the experience sheet helps the students break down their goals into more easily managed steps.

Allow 10 to 15 minutes for the students to write down the steps for each goal. While they are writing, offer assistance. This task will be foreign to most students and they will need guidance in formulating the steps. Again, you can add significantly to this activity by sitting with each student and assisting in the development of the steps—particularly if the goal pertains to success in your class.

Direct the students to keep their experience sheets and refer to them daily as they work toward their goals. Review the progress of the students weekly or biweekly in class. Lead a discussion after each review.

Discussion Questions:

1. How do you feel about having completed steps toward your goal?
2. If you haven't completed any steps, how do you feel about falling short? What can you do about it?
3. When you need the help of others to achieve a goal, how can you build in that requirement as part of your plan?

You Can Reach Your Goals!

Student Experience Sheet

PART 1

What are goals?

A goal is an end, home base, the final destination, what you are aiming for. Goals can center on having something—clothes, a car, money—or they can center on achieving—finishing school, going to college, having a career, becoming famous.

Short-term and long-range goals

Short-term goals include making phone calls, finishing your homework, cleaning your room, doing your chores, or making plans for the weekend. Long-range goals might include planning a trip for next summer, deciding to go to a trade school, a community college, or a university; saving money to buy something special; or making plans for your future career.

Goals are written in special ways. They are:
1. Positive (They contain no negative words.)
2. Personal (They're about us, not others.)
3. Written as though they are happening now or have already happened.

Researchers tell us that when we write goals in this way we connect with the part of our brain that tells us what we need to do. Have you ever wanted to make something? You may remember that after you decided what you wanted to make (your goal) you started thinking of things you needed to have and/or do in order to attain your goal. You even figured out the order in which the steps needed to be completed. Perhaps you wrote down the steps. The more often you set goals in this way, the more often you get what you want.

Take a look at your goals.

In the following spaces, take a few minutes to write down some of your goals. Check whether each goal is short-term or long-range, and write in the date by which you plan to accomplish it.

Goal #1_____

_____

Short Term_____ Long Range_____ Target Date_____

Goal #2 _____

_____

Short Term _____ Long Range_____ Target Date_____

Goal #3 _____

_____

Short Term_____ Long Range_____ Target Date_____

Now answer these questions about one of your goals:
1. Is this goal one you decided to set, or did someone else influence you to set it?
2. How do you feel about having this goal?
3. Is this a realistic goal for you (one that you can attain)?
4. What frustrations or conflicts were involved in setting this goal?
5. What risks are involved in reaching this goal?
6. With whom did you consult before you decided on this goal?

Describe roadblocks that might interfere with your reaching this goal. List strategies for overcoming each roadblock.

	Roadblocks	Strategies
Goal #1	_____	_____
	_____	_____
Goal #2	_____	_____
	_____	_____
Goal #3	_____	_____
	_____	_____

PART 2

Goal Achievement Score Sheet

Goal #1 _____

_____

Steps Toward Achieving My Goal:	Review Date	Achieved	Not Achieved
1. _____			
2. _____			
3. _____			
4. _____			

Goal #2 _____

_____

Steps Toward Achieving My Goal:	Review Date	Achieved	Not Achieved
1. _____			
2. _____			
3. _____			
4. _____			

Goal #3 _____

_____

Steps Toward Achieving My Goal:	Review Date	Achieved	Not Achieved
1. _____			
2. _____			
3. _____			
4. _____			

Tips for Setting Goals
Student Experience Sheet

1. <u>Goals must be clear and describe exactly what you want or will do.</u>

2. <u>Goals must be personal</u>. They must be about you, not someone else.

3. <u>Goals must be measurable.</u> You need to know when you have achieved your goal.

4. <u>Goals must have realistic time limits.</u>

5. <u>Goals must be manageable.</u> Divide big goals into several smaller, attainable goals or tasks. This will enable you to experience results in a shorter period to time.

6. <u>Goals must be stated in positive rather than negative terms:</u> (I *will* do something rather than I *won't* do something.)

7. <u>Goals must be written down.</u> People are more likely to achieve goals that are in writing. Written goals can be reviewed regularly, and have more power. Like a contract with yourself, they are harder to neglect or forget.

Supporting Goals Through Visualizations and Affirmations

Experience Sheets and Discussion

Objectives:

The students will:

—learn how to use visualization and affirmations in goal setting.

Materials:

one copy each of the experience sheets, "What You See Is What You Get" and "What You Say is What You Get," for each student; chalkboard or chart paper

Directions:

Write the terms *Visualization* and *Affirmation* on the board. Explain to the students that visualization and affirmation are important techniques that can help them achieve their goals. Ask the students to help you define both terms. Write their ideas on the board and, if you like, add symbols and simple drawings to illustrate the concept of visualizations. At some point, read the following paragraphs aloud and incorporate any

concepts they contain that the students have not included in their definitions.

<u>Visualizations</u> are the pictures of achievement we have of ourselves. These pictures greatly affect the outcomes we produce. If we *see* ourselves succeeding and attaining our goals, we very likely will. If, on the other hand, we have no image of success or create an image of failure, we very likely will fail.

<u>Affirmations</u> are the words and statements we use to support our goals and pictures of achievement. Whatever we tell ourselves about our ability to achieve our goals affects the subconscious mind. The subconscious mind doesn't distinguish between that which is real and that which is imagined. It sets about creating *whatever* we will tell it. Positive affirmations are a systematic way of programming the subconscious for success.

Share with the students a personal experience in which the skills of visualization and affirmation have helped you. Next, ask volunteers to share a personal experience in which they succeeded at something after having used some form of visualization and/or affirmation.

Have the students complete the experience sheets, "What You See Is What You Get" and "What You Say Is What You Get." When they have finished, lead a culminating discussion.

Discussion Questions:

1. How did you feel about creating the treasure map?
2. How has the experience changed your perception of your goal?
3. How did you feel while creating affirmations?
4. What was hardest about writing affirmations? What was easiest?
5. How have your feelings about your ability to reach your goals changed as a result of writing affirmations?
6. How can you discipline yourself to use your visualization and affirmations often?

The greatest discovery of my generation is that human beings, by changing the inner attitudes of their minds, can change the outer aspects of their lives.

—William James

What You See Is What You Get

Student Experience Sheet

What do you think William James meant when he made that statement? James may not have been familiar with the term, but what he was talking about was *visualization*. Visualizing is something everybody does, every day. When you daydream, think about someone you know, or remember a place you visited in the past, you are visualizing. And you can make the technique of visualization *work for you*. You can use it to help achieve your goals. Here's how:

As clearly and realistically as possible, visualize your desired goal as if it were already reality. Hang this picture in your mental gallery, and look at it often. Your visualization will help you stay focused on your goal and able to take advantage of all the opportunities that come along that may help you reach your goal.

Create a Treasure Map

Paint or draw a treasure map—an actual, physical picture of your goal. Make it a clear, sharp image that you can focus on. If you like, instead of (or in addition to) drawing your treasure map, cut out pictures and words from magazines and make a collage. Follow these guidelines:

1. Do a treasure map for a single goal—don't try to include several goals.
2. Put YOU in the picture. Use a photo or draw an image of yourself.
3. Show the complete and glorious outcome of your goal.
4. Use lots of color. Color can have quite an impact on your mind.
5. Make the size of your treasure map work for you—whether you want to carry it in your notebook or hang on your wall. Have **FUN!!!**

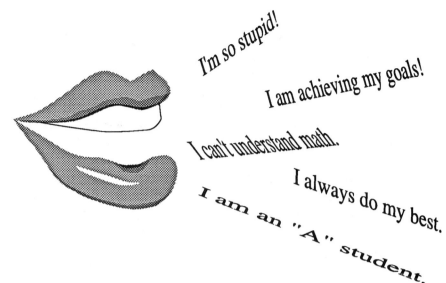

I'm so stupid!

I am achieving my goals!

I can't understand math.

I always do my best.

I am an "A" student.

What You Say Is What You Get
Student Experience Sheet

Affirmations are the words you use to trigger positive pictures and feelings within you. An affirmation is a strong, positive statement that *describes something as FACT*. Affirmations work in the subconscious mind, by replacing negative statements with positive statements. Affirmations help you to achieve your goals by:

—stimulating your subconscious to be continuously alert to situations that will further your goal.

—signaling the conscious mind to actively engage in those situations.

In order for affirmations to work, they must be written in a special way.

1. Affirmations must be **personal** and **under your control.** You cannot affirm or alter situations that you do not control.

2. Write affirmations in **positive language.** You must use vivid words and phrases to describe what you want. For example, don't say "I am no longer unorganized." Instead say, "I am a neat and organized person."

3. Write affirmations in the **present tense.** The subconscious mind only operates in the "now." If you create affirmations in the future tense, your subconscious will never get there.

4. Write affirmations as if you have **already achieved** your goal. Don't say "I can." "I have" and "I am" are more powerful. By describing your goal as already achieved, you are clearly conveying the desired outcome to your subconscious.

5. Begin affirmations with words that **convey action and emotion**. Words like "I easily," and "I quickly" convey action. Words like "I confidently" and "I enthusiastically" show emotion. Action and feeling words make your affirmation more believable and attractive.

6. Affirmations must be **realistic**. Develop affirmations that aim for excellence not perfection. Write affirmations that have a good chance of happening.

Here are some examples of positive, well written affirmations:
I express myself well and I know others respect my point of view.
I enthusiastically do my homework every night.
I am happily involved in a variety of interests in my school and community.
I willingly help my family members in any way I can.
I am a good friend and I enjoy my relationships.

Now, think back to the goals you wrote in an earlier activity. Follow the guidelines outlined above, and write two affirmations for each goal.
Goal #1:
Affirmation 1: _____

Affirmation 2: _____

Goal #2:
Affirmation 1: _____

Affirmation 2: _____

Goal #3:
Affirmation 1: _____

Affirmation 2: _____

Now put your affirmations to work.
• Read your affirmations several times each day.
• When you read the affirmations, look at or think of your treasure map at the same time. The words and picture reinforce each other.
• Enjoy the positive feeling of accomplishment each time you repeat your affirmation.

The degree to which your affirmation impacts your subconscious depends on *how* you use it and *how often* you use it. Compare these percentages.

Just reading the affirmation	=	10% impact
Reading and visualizing	=	55% impact
Reading, visualizing and *feeling*	=	100% impact

Visualize and repeat your affirmations throughout the day. Keep your subconscious focused on your goal and it will move you along the path to achievement.

The Value of Rewards

Experience Sheet and Discussion

Objectives:

The students will:
—describe the importance of rewarding themselves for goal attainment.
—write down one reward in connection with each of their goals.

Materials:

one copy of the experience sheet, "A Pat on The Back," for each student

Directions:

Introduce the experience sheet "A Pat On The Back" by saying something like: *An important and often overlooked element of goal setting is the reward. Rewards should be established during the planning process and should be coupled with both short-term and long-range goals. Rewarding yourself for achieving a short term-goal will give you the motivation you need to continue working toward other short-term as well as long-range goals.*

Anything you enjoy or value can be used as a reward. Plan to buy yourself a new CD or book, or have dinner at your favorite restaurant. Rewards, like goals, should be realistic. By choosing a reward that is either unattainable or unaffordable, you will be undermining your ability to achieve the associated goal.

Distribute the experience sheets. Give the students a few minutes to transfer their goal statements from the experience sheet, "You Can Reach Your Goals." Then ask the students to think of a realistic yet desirable reward for each goal.

When all of the students have completed the experience sheet, have them break into groups of three to five and take turns sharing their rewards. Allow about 10 minutes for interaction. Then lead a culminating class discussion.

Discussion Questions:

1. How do rewards help the process of goal setting and attainment?

2. What is one reward that you have given yourself in the past for achieving a goal? Did that reward encourage you to pursue more goals?

3. What are some distinctions between a reward that you give yourself and one that you get as a natural consequence of achieving a goal, like recognition or a good feeling? Which is more important?

4. How can we support each other in achieving our goals?

A Pat on the Back
Student Experience Sheet

When you have set and accomplished a goal, congratulate yourself! Reward yourself, too! Think of one nice thing you can do for yourself when you have achieved each of your goals. Describe it here:

Goal #1: _____

How I will reward myself: _____

_____

Goal #2: _____

How I will reward myself: _____

_____

Goal #3: _____

How I will reward myself: _____

_____

One of My Goals Is...

A Goal-Reinforcement Activity

Objectives:

The students will:

—practice dealing with imagined obstacles to the goal.

—identify steps to attaining the goal.

Directions:

Locate an area large enough to accommodate groups of three students, allowing ample space between groups. Divide the students randomly into groups of three. Have them decide who will be **A**, **B**, and **C**. (Extra **C**'s may be assigned to some groups.)

Explain the procedure to the students: *Person **A**, you are the "goal-setter," and will state a goal that you want to achieve. Person **B**, you are the "discourager." You will come up with all the problems, obstacles, and roadblocks that could make achieving the goal difficult. Person **C**, you are the "encourager." You will offer ideas and solutions for achieving the goal. You will help remove the roadblocks. Offer any good ideas you can think of to help the goal-setter be successful. After a few minutes, I'll call time and tell you to switch roles. We will do three rounds, so that everyone can play all three roles.*

Choose two volunteers and demonstrate the rotation process and the goal-setter/discourager/encourager interaction. Provide examples of goal statements, positive statements, and negative statements.

Lead the activity through three rounds. Circulate. After everyone has had a turn in each role, facilitate a class discussion.

Discussion Questions:

1. What obstacles or roadblocks were mentioned most often?
3. Why do we have dialogues like this inside ourselves?
3. Do you think this activity will help you accomplish your goal? How?

Decision Making

Understanding the processes and influences that shape decision making and influence problem solving are skills possessed and exercised by effective people of all ages. The quality of a decision is frequently determined by the degree of conscious effort that has gone into its making. Good decision making involves using information about values, goals, influences, alternatives, and probable consequences to make choices that achieve desirable outcomes. Problem solving is often a larger process that involves multiple decisions.

Young people make scores of decisions daily. Many of these decisions are habitual and automatic. Others deserve considerable thought and study, whether they receive it or not. In social studies classes, students learn about decisions that determined the course of history. In this unit, students learn processes that help them determine the course of their own lives.

Activities ask students to assess previous decisions, and to help each other make current decisions and solve existing problems. In the process, students are guided through step-by-step problem-solving and decision-making processes.

Decisions, Decisions!

Experience Sheet and Discussion

Objectives:

The students will:

—understand and describe how decisions are influenced.

—develop and practice a process for effective decision making.

Materials:

one copy of the experience sheet, "The De-cision-Making Process," for each student; chalkboard or chart paper

Directions:

Distribute the experience sheets. Read through the decision-making steps with the students, examining each one. Here are some suggestions to discuss and questions to ask:

• **(Step 2)** Knowing what is important to you and what you want to accomplish involves such things as likes/dislikes, values, and interests. Most important, it involves having goals. As the Cheshire Cat said to Alice: " If you don't know where you're going, any road will take you there."

• **(Step 3)** You can get information by talking to people, visiting places, watching TV, and reading. Once you have the information, you must be able to evaluate it. If two people tell you to do opposite things, how are you going to know which is right? What if neither is right? What if both are righ⁴?

• **(Step 5)** Look into the future. Ask yourself what would be the probable outcome if you chose each of the alternatives available. Practice with the students by asking them to predict their future based on these questions:

What would happen if:
—you did not go to college?
—you never got married?
—you dropped out of school?
—you became temporarily disabled?
—you became a professional rock singer?
—you decided never to drink alcohol?
—you decided not to have children?

How did you make your predictions? What information did you use?

• (**Step 6**) When you reach the decision point, don't procrastinate. If you've done a good job on the other steps, you can choose the best alternative with confidence. Remember, if you don't choose, someone else may choose for you.

• (**Step 7**) Not every decision requires an action plan, but the big ones usually do. The decision to attend a 4-year college in another state won't come true unless you make it. And that means more decisions. Can you think what they are?

Give the students time to complete the experience sheet. (If you run out of time, let them complete it as homework.)

Have the students choose partners and take turns sharing their decisions and decision-making process. Facilitate a culminating discussion.

Discussion Questions:

1. What did you learn about decision-making from this activity?
2. What can happen if you put off making a decision?
3. Why is it important to know your interests and values when making decisions?
4. How can having goals help you make decisions?

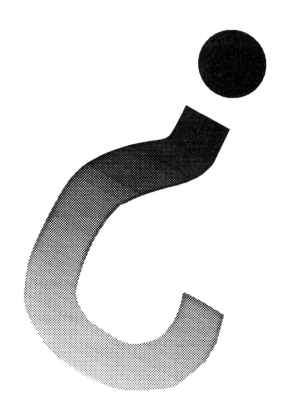

The Decision-Making Process
Student Experience Sheet

The decision-making process involves using what you know (or can learn) to get what you want.

Here are some steps to follow when you have a decision to make:
1. Recognize and define the decision to be made.
2. Know what is important to you—your values—and what you want to accomplish—your goal.
3. Study the information you have already; obtain and study new information, too.
4. List all of your alternatives.
5. List the advantages and disadvantages of each alternative.
6. Make a decision.
7. Develop a plan for carrying out your decision.

Now let's see how the process really works. Think of a decision that you need to make in the next month. Define it here:

_____

What is your goal concerning this decision?_____

_____

What kinds of things that are important in your life (your values) might affect or be affected by this decision?

_____

_____

What kinds of information do you have or need?

Things to think about: _____

_____

People to talk to:_____

_____

Things to read: _____

_____

Things to do: _____

_____

What are your alternatives and their advantages and disadvantages?

Alternative: _____

Advantages _____   Disadvantages _____

_____   _____

Alternative: _____

Advantages _____   Disadvantages _____

_____   _____

Alternative: _____

Advantages _____   Disadvantages _____

_____   _____

Decision Point! Which alternative (or combination of alternatives) has the best chance of producing the outcome you want?

What is your plan for putting this decision into action? Describe each step:

1. _____

_____

2. _____

_____

3. _____

_____

4. _____

_____

5. _____

_____

6. _____

_____

7. _____

_____

8. _____

_____

9. _____

_____

Decisions and Outcomes

Assessment and Discussion

Objectives:
The students will:
—understand and describe how decisions are influenced.
—state the outcomes and possible consequences of specific decisions.

Materials:
one copy of the experience sheet, "More About Decisions...," for each student

Directions:
Begin by defining *decision making* as a process in which a person selects from two or more choices. Point out that:

• A decision is not necessary unless there is more than one course of action to consider.

• *Not* deciding is making a decision.

• Two people facing similar decisions create unique outcomes because they want different things.

• Learning decision-making skills increases the possibility that a person can have what he or she wants.

• Each decision is limited by what a person is *able* to do and what he or she is *willing* to do. *Ability* is increased by having more alternatives. *Willingness* is usually determined by values and goals.

Distribute the experience sheets. Allow a few minutes for their completion.

To reinforce the differences between decisions and outcomes, play a game with the students. Introduce the game by saying: *I'm going to play a game of chance with you. You must make the decision whether or not to play. I am going to flip a coin. Before I flip* it, I want you to write down on a slip of paper whether the coin is "heads" or "tails." Put your name on your paper, and give it to me. After I flip the coin, I will go through the papers and give every student who guessed correctly five extra points for the day. Those who guessed incorrectly will get no extra points. Remember, you do not have to play.

Play the game. Afterwards, ask the students these questions:
—How many chose to play the game?
—How many chose not to play the game?
—If you chose to play the game, but guessed incorrectly, was that a poor decision or a poor outcome? (outcome)
—If you played the game and guessed correctly, was that a good decision or a good outcome? (both)
—If you chose not to play the game, was that a good or a poor decision? Why?

Conclude the activity with further discussion.

Discussion Questions:
1. What did you find out about your "worst decision" from this activity?
2. What is the difference between decisions and outcomes?
3. If your decision was truly bad, how could you have made a better one?
4. What kinds of decisions require study and thought?
5. How can having decision-making skills help you in school? ...in your job? ...after high school?

More About
Decisions

Student Experience Sheet

Write down all the decisions that you can remember making so far today.
For example, you probably made decisions about what to wear, what to eat, how to
spend your breaks and with whom. You may have made decisions about whether
to go to class, how to approach an assignment, what to say to someone, and whether
to tell the truth. Include all types of decisions on your list.

Decisions

1. _____

2. _____

3. _____

4. _____

5. _____

6. _____

7. _____

Now go back through your list of decisions and code each one with a number from this scale.

    0 = I have no control over this type of decision; it is dictated by others.
    1 = This type of decision is automatic, routine, or habitual.
    2 = I occasionally think about this type of decision.
    3 = I think about this type of decision, but I don't study it.
    4 = I study this type of decision somewhat.
    5 = I study this type of decision a lot.

What does this exercise tell you about how you make most of your decisions?

_____

What is the worst decision you ever made? Write a brief description of it here: _____

_____

_____

Decision or Outcome? Next time you're tempted to kick yourself over a "bad" decision, consider this:

- When you say that a decision is poor, you probably mean the *result* or *outcome* is not what you wanted.

- Good decision making minimizes the possibility of getting bad outcomes, but it doesn't eliminate the possibility.

- A *decision* is the act of choosing among several possibilities based on your judgments.

- An *outcome* is the result, consequence, or aftermath of the decision.

- You have direct control over the decision, but *not* over the outcome.

- A good decision does not guarantee a good outcome, but it does increase the chances of a good outcome.

Go back and look at your "worst" decision again. Was it really a bad decision, or was it a reasonable decision with a bad outcome?

Factoring a Decision
Experience Sheet and Discussion

Objectives:
The students will:
—describe and analyze a recent decision.
—discuss factors that affect decision making.
—explain how to increase alternatives during decision making.

Materials:
one copy of the experience sheet, "Increasing Your Alternatives," for each student; chalkboard or chart paper

Directions:
Begin the activity by reviewing concepts related to decision making that were covered in previous activities. Elicit contributions from the students and write notes on the board. Be sure to make the following points:

1. A decision is not necessary unless there is more than one course of action to choose from.

2. Not deciding is making a decision.

3. Learning decision-making skills increases the possibility that I can have what I want.

4. Each decision is limited by what I am *able* to do. For example, if I cannot drive a car, I cannot choose between walking and driving.

5. The more alternatives I know about, the more I am *able* to do. For example, if I am unaware of a particular college, I cannot include it among my alternatives when deciding where to go to school.

6. Each decision is also limited by what I am *willing* to do.

7. What I am willing to do is usually determined by my values, beliefs, preferences, and past experiences.

Distribute the experience sheets. Go over the items on the sheet and answer any questions. Then give the students about 10 minutes to complete the sheet.

Have the students form small groups and share their responses. When they have finished, lead a culminating class discussion.

Discussion Questions:

1. What did you learn about decision making from this activity?
2. What can you do to increase your alternatives in a decision-making situation?
3. What kinds of things determine your willingness to try a particular alternative?
4. When your willingness is more a product of low self-confidence than of values, how can you overcome that roadblock?
5. How do your beliefs affect decision making? Your attitudes? Your previous experiences?

Increasing Your Alternatives
Student Experience Sheet

Think of a decision you need to make. Describe it here:_____

a_____

a_____

What are you *able* to do in this situation? Write down as many realistic alternatives as you can think of.

1. _____

2. _____

3. _____

4. _____

5. _____

Go back and circle all of the alternatives you are *willing* to try.

One of the best ways to increase your chances of making a good decision is to increase your alternatives. Write down as many ideas as you can think of for increasing your alternatives.

1. _____

_____

2. _____

_____

3. _____

_____

4. _____

_____

5. _____

_____

6. _____

_____

7. _____

_____

8. _____

_____

9. _____

_____

Remember: In decision making, information is your biggest ally.

The Key Word Is Choice

Experience Sheet and Discussion

Objectives:
The students will:
—examine the elements of choice and responsibility in decision making.
—describe decisions involving frustration, procrastination, and risk.

Materials:
one copy of the experience sheet, "The Choice is Yours," for each student; chalkboard or chart paper

Directions:
Distribute the experience sheets. Give the students about 15 minutes to complete the sheet. Than have them form groups of three to five, and share their responses to the questions.

After the groups have finished sharing, facilitate a class discussion. Focus on the elements of responsibility and choice in decision making.

Discussion Questions:
1. Why is it sometimes difficult to take the initiative concerning decisions that affect us?
2. When you were a child, your parents or guardians made many decisions for you. What affect might that have on your ability to assume responsibility for decision making now?
3. What kind of decision is "putting off" or not making a decision?
4. When you have to choose between two equally attractive alternatives, how can you weigh them more carefully?
5. Some people love to make decisions that involve big risks. Others like to play it safe. How can you determine how much risk is right for you, so that you won't get in over your head?

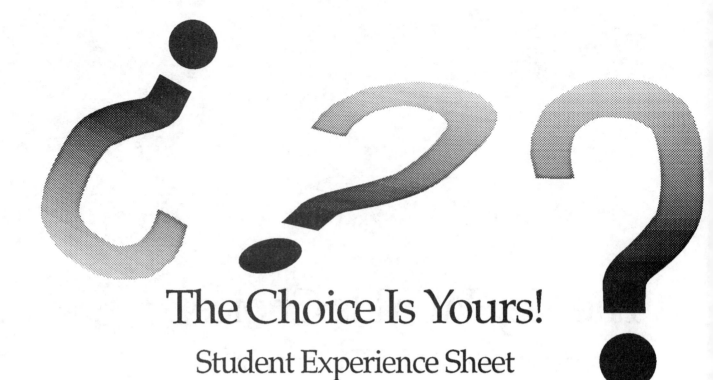

The Choice Is Yours!

Student Experience Sheet

Dan starts a class he doesn't enjoy much, and after a couple of days he says to himself, "I'm not interested in anything being covered in this class. I don't have to take it to graduate, so I'm going to transfer to a class that I'll be able to use, one that I'll enjoy." And he does.

Maria has similar feelings about a class. But after thinking it over, she decides that since the class is in her major field, she'll stick with it. As the semester continues, Maria finds that the class gets more interesting.

Suzanne feels the same way about a class she signed up for, but doesn't transfer to another one. She doesn't want to disappoint her parents or cause anyone to think she isn't capable of handling the class.

Dan, Suzanne, and Maria all face a similar situation, but each reacts differently. Suzanne's decision is based on what she imagines other people will think, rather than her own needs. Dan and Maria decide to do different things, but both of them make thoughtful decisions based on their own needs and values.

Think of a decision you made recently that worked out well. *What was it?*

_____

_____

_____

_____

_____

Who and/or what influenced your decision?

___ your needs (things you can't get along without)

___ your values (what you like)

___ your goals (what you want to accomplish)

___ other people (Who?)

___ advertising

___ other (What?)

Sometimes making decisions can be frustrating.

For weeks, Ryan has been working on his car. he has spent all his money and every available hour getting it fixed up for a custom car show. Now, the day before the show, some of his friends invite him to go with them to the river tomorrow. Ryan really enjoys going to the river, but he wants to enter his car in the show, too. Both things are happening on the same day. It makes him mad that he has to choose between two things he wants.

Has anything like this ever happened to you? How did you feel at the time?

_____

What did you do? _____

_____

Sometimes we decide not to decide.

The coach asks Tom if he wants to be on the track team, which makes Tom feel great, except that he is nervous about being the newest and least experienced person on the team. So Tom puts off making a decision. Accidentally (on purpose) he forgets to let the coach know by the deadline. *A day or two later Tom says to himself, "Too bad I forgot about notifying Coach that I wanted to be on the track team. Oh, well."*

Have you ever put off making a decision? If you could get that day back, what would you do this time?

_____

_____

Sometimes decisions are risky.

Sheila thinks she wants to go to college, but she isn't sure what it will be like. She's been planning to go to a nearby community college for two years while continuing to live at home. Then she finds out that she could live with her aunt in the city and go to a well-known four-year college. Sheila doesn't know if she really wants to leave home yet, if she wants to live with her aunt, or which college will be the better choice for her.

What do you think Sheila should do?

___ Live at home and go to the community college.

___ Live with her aunt and go to the four-year college.

___ Get a lot more information before making a decision.

What types of information does Sheila need? **List at least three categories here:**

Information about _____

Information about _____

Information about _____

Steps for Solving a Problem Responsibly
Student Experience Sheet and Discussion

Objectives:
The students will:
—understand and describe how decisions are influenced.
—develop and practice a process for effective problem solving.

Materials:
one copy of the experience sheet, "Steps for Solving a Problem Responsibly,"for each student; chalkboard or chart paper

Directions:
Distribute the experience sheets. Have the students read each step in the problem-solving process with you while writing notes on their sheet. Generate discussion after each step by asking appropriate open-ended questions. Introduce a personal example (a problem that you need to solve) and take it through the process as part of the discussion. If time permits, go back through the process

a second time, using as an example a problem described by one of the students.

Discussion Questions:
Stop all blaming
1. What happens when you get bogged down in the blaming game?

2. What are people who constantly blame others for their problems trying to avoid?

3. How is blaming others the same as giving away your power?

Define the problem
1. Why is it so important to know exactly what the problem is?

2. Why does it matter whether it's your problem or someone else's?

3. When should people not be left to solve their own problems?

4. What can happen when a person gets all worked up about a problem that isn't even theirs?

Consider asking for help
1. When is it wise to ask for help?

2. Who gets to decide what kind of help you need?

3. If what you want is information or advice, and instead the person tries to solve the problem for you, what can you do?

Think of alternative solutions.
1. What is the advantage of thinking of alternatives?

2. If you can't think of more than one or two alternatives, what should you definitely do before making a decision?

3. How does collecting information expand your alternatives?

Evaluate the alternatives.
1. What are some ways of collecting information?

2. Why not just do the first thing that comes to mind?

3. Why is it important to imagine what will happen as a result of trying each alternative?

Make a decision.
1. If you still can't make a decision, which steps in the process could you return to? (2., 4., 5., and 3., in that order. The problem may be incorrectly defined; you may need to gather additional information; the consequences may need further consideration; or help may be called for.)

Follow through
1. Why stick to a decision?

2. What can you do if the solution doesn't work or more problems come up?

3. How can you evaluate your decision?

4. What's an example of a big problem in our society that used to be a much smaller problem with a relatively easy solution?

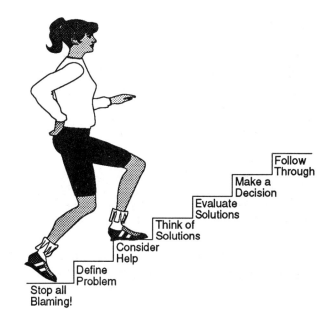

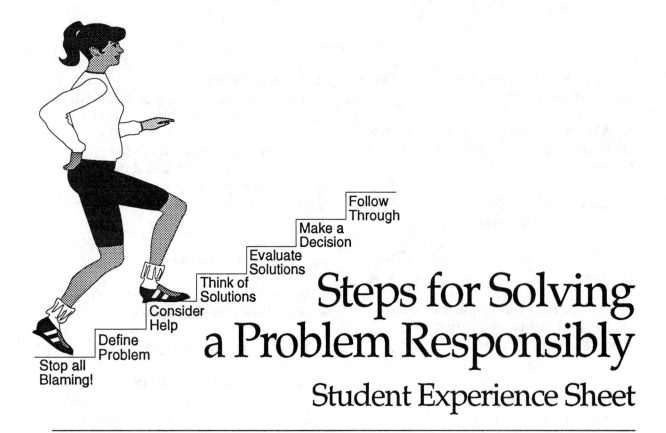

Stop all Blaming!

Define Problem

Consider Help

Think of Solutions

Evaluate Solutions

Make a Decision

Follow Through

Steps for Solving a Problem Responsibly
Student Experience Sheet

1. Stop all blaming.
Blaming someone (including myself) for the problem will not solve it. If I really want to solve the problem, I need to put my energy into working out a solution. Blaming myself and others is a waste of time.

2. Define the problem.
I need to ask myself two questions to help me get started. "What exactly is the problem?" and "Whose problem is it?" If I find that it's not my problem, the best thing I can do is let the people who "own" the problem solve it themselves. Or I can ask, "How can I help you?"

3. Consider asking for help.
Once I'm sure I "own" the problem and know what it is, I may choose to ask someone for help. For example, I may decide to talk over the problem with someone I trust.

4. Think of alternative solutions.
I need to ask myself, "What are some things I could do about this?" I need to think of as many reasonable ideas for solving the problem as I can. To do this, I will probably need to collect some information.

5. Evaluate the alternatives.
For each idea I come up with, I need to ask myself, "What will happen to me and the other people involved if I try this one?" I need to be very honest with myself. If I don't know how someone else will be affected, I need to ask that person, "How will you feel about it if I..."

6. Make a decision.
I need to choose the alternative that has the best chance of succeeding. If my solution is a responsible one, it will not hurt anyone unnecessarily—and it will probably work.

7. Follow through.
I'll stick to my decision for a reasonable length of time. If the decision doesn't work, I'll try another alternative. If it works, but causes more problems in the process, I'll start all over again to solve them. And I'll try not to blame myself or anybody else for those problems.

Youth Can Solve Problems
Current-Events Research, Brainstorming, and Discussion

Objectives:
The students will:
— select and summarize a current-events article dealing with an important issue or event.
— generate solutions to a current-events problem presented by the teacher.
— in small groups, achieve consensus on a solution to the problem.

Materials:
current-events articles (brought by the students from home); an article to read to the students

Preparation:
Ask the students to cut a current-events article from a newspaper or news magazine and bring it to school on the day of the activity. Require that the articles deal with an issue or event of some importance. Bring an article of your own dealing with a problem for which creative solutions are obviously needed.

Directions:
Talk to the students about the importance of being well-informed. Explain that the community, the nation, and the world are made up of individuals such as they. The world is shaped by the interest and participation of individual people working together. People build, produce, feed, govern, and educate. In the process, they create conflicts and problems, which they also must solve. Ask the students what kinds of issues, events, and problems they discovered while reading the newspaper. Ask two or three volunteers to briefly tell the class about their articles.

Have the students share their article with a partner. Allow about 5 minutes for this. Then read *your* article aloud to the class. Define terms used in the article, and discuss the problem. Ask these questions:
—*What is the problem?*
—*Whose problem is it?*

Announce that through group discussion, the students are going to come up with solutions to the problem described in the article. Have the students form groups of three to five. Give them 1 minute to choose a leader and a recorder. Then announce that the groups will have 10 minutes to brainstorm solutions to the problem.

Call time after 10 minutes, and have the groups discuss and evaluate their suggestions, one at a time. Their task is to choose one solution to present to the class. Suggest that they answer these questions:
—*Will this solution solve the problem?*
—*Can this solution actually be done?*
—*Will combining any suggestions make a better solution?*

Allow a few more minutes for discussion. Urge the groups to use the process of consensus-seeking to make their decision. Have the group leaders report the class. Then lead a culminating discussion.

Discussion Questions:
1. What was the hardest part about finding a solution to this problem? What was the easiest part?
2. If your group was not able to come to a decision, why not?
3. How were disagreements or conflicts handled in your group?
4. Is there any way for individuals or nations to avoid having problems? Explain.
5. How will learning to solve problems here in the classroom help prepare us to solve them in the outside world?

Dear Matilda ...

Creative Writing and Discussion

Objectives:
The students will:
—write about a real problem.
—describe possible solutions to a problem.
—identify any overlap between serious and humorous alternatives.

Materials:
paper, a collection box (for problems), and bulletin boards for posting letters and responses

Directions:
Read aloud a column from the daily paper to which readers write with problems and in which the columnist offers advice and solutions. If available, read a spoof on an advice column from a source such as *National Lampoon* or *Mad* magazine.

Ask the students to write a brief letter to "Matilda." Assure them that Matilda will respond. Explain that the letter should consist of a request for advice concerning a real problem, present or past. If the students can't think of a problem of their own to describe, tell them its okay to describe someone else's problem, as long as they know enough about it to be specific. Ask the students to sign their letters with fictitious names, and drop them into the collection box.

Have each student reach into the box and draw out a letter. Instruct the students to prepare two answers to the letter—one that is serious and sincere and one that is humorous. Allow the students to consult with each other in dyads or triads to generate ideas for thoughtful and amusing responses. The rest of the period can be devoted to writing. Ask the students to sign their real names to both responses.

Collect and read the letters and responses. Correct the responses only, and offer the students an opportunity to rewrite them. Have the students post their letters and responses on a class bulletin board. Give the students time to circulate and read each other's letters and responses.

Discussion Questions:
1. How did your serious and humorous approaches to problem solving differ?
2. Did thinking in a humorous vein produce any creative alternatives that could actually be considered? What were they?
3. What kinds of questions did you, as "Matilda," want to ask your correspondent about his/her problem?
4. How did having limited information affect your problem-solving ability?

Imagining Alternatives
Guided Imagery and Discussion

Objectives:
The students will:
—privately define a problem and imagine alternatives for solving it.
—practice steps in the decision-making process.

Materials:
cassette tape player and tape of soft, relaxing music (optional)

Directions:
Announce that you are going to lead the students in a guided imagery designed to demonstrate the power of imagination in evaluating alternative solutions to a problem. If you are using music, start the tape at a low volume. Read the following script slowly and in a pleasant, soothing voice. Pause frequently to allow the students sufficient time to follow your directions.

Get comfortable in your chair... Uncross your arms and legs... Close your eyes... Take a deep breath... As you let it out, think back to an experience you had in which you wish you had acted differently... The experience can have to do with anything... Maybe you made the decision to do something that you knew was wrong... and you wish you hadn't said or done what you did . . . Maybe you were silent and you wish you had spoken up... Maybe the decision seemed right at the time, but turned out badly... (Pause 15 seconds.)... I'd like you to go back to that situation now... Remember where you were and watch yourself as though it were happening on a stage... Just silently remember... (Pause 15 seconds.) . . . Who was there?... What were you doing?... What were others doing? . . . What were people saying to each other? ... Remember exactly what you did that you wish you had done differently... Perhaps at the time you felt you had no other choice. . . (Pause 15 seconds.) . . . Let that scene become very small in your mind. . . As the sounds fade away, create a new scene. . . Let your imagination picture how you wish you had acted in the situation. . . how you could have moved and what you could have said. . . Take a few minutes to play the scene out to its conclusion. . . (Pause 30 seconds.) . . .

Now think of a problem that you have today. . . something that is bothering you. . . a decision that you have to make. . . Gradually set this new scene on the stage in your mind. . . Picture the other people involved. . . See yourself not only in the scene but as the director of the scene. . . Give yourself a director's chair and imagine that you are about to shoot two or three versions of the scene. . . to see which works best. . . (Pause 15 seconds.) . . . Roll the cameras on the first version. . . Imagine every detail of how you could solve the problem. . . (Pause 30 seconds.) . . . Now, if you need to, change the actors and the scenery and get ready to play a second version of the scene. . . What is another way that you could solve this problem? . . . Picture every detail of the action. . . (Pause 30 seconds.) . . . Cut the action and change the scene one last time. . . Set the stage for a third possible solution to your problem. . . Get all the actors in their places. . . Now play the scene. . . (Pause 30 seconds.) . . .

Now remember each of the three scenes you created. . . and select the one that worked best. . . (Pause 10 seconds.) . . . Get up out of the director's chair and step into the scene. . . into your role. . . and play it again as if you are actually doing it, not seeing it. . . Feel yourself moving. . . hear yourself speaking. . . Intensify every feeling and action . . . Take all the time you need to fully experience the solution you've chosen. . . (Pause 40 seconds.) . . . Know that you always have the power to choose the best course of action. . . When you are ready, come back to this room. . . Listen to the sounds here. . . and open your eyes.

Lead a summary discussion, focusing on the process, not the problems or solutions of the students.

Discussion Questions:
1. How did this process work for you?
2. What is the value of giving imaginary life to different alternatives?
3. What part of the process would you change to make it work better for you?
4. How could you utilize this process in the future?

Have a Heart!
Decision-Making Exercise

Objectives:

The students will:

—make a shared decision concerning a difficult issue.

—describe their shared decision-making process.

—describe how values and attitudes affect decision making.

Materials:

one copy of the "Patient Waiting List" for each small group; writing materials

Directions:

Announce that the students are going to have an opportunity to make group decisions concerning a highly-charged, imaginary situation in which individual values and attitudes may play a significant role.

Ask the students to form groups of five to seven. Give each group a copy of the "Patient Waiting List," and suggest that every group choose a recorder.

Read the situation and the list of patients to the groups:

Situation

You are surgeons at a large hospital. Your committee must make a very important decision. Seven patients need a heart transplant. There is only one heart donor at this time. All of the patients are eligible to receive the heart. All are physically able. And all have compatible blood and tissue typing. Which patient would you choose to receive the heart? Why? Your committee must agree on the choice.

(You may wish to acknowledge that most recipients of organ transplants are now managed by a nationwide computer network, which largely removes such difficult decisions from the hands of the surgeons themselves. Ask the students to participate as if such a system had not yet been developed. Also, remind the students that patients who do not receive this heart will not *automatically* die. Some (not all) will probably survive until another donor is available.)

Patient Waiting List

• 31-year-old male; Black; brain surgeon at the height of his career; no children

• 12-year-old female; Vietnamese; accomplished violinist, blind

• 40-year-old male; Hispanic; teacher; two children

• 15 year female; White; unmarried; 6-months pregnant

• 35-year-old male; Hispanic; Roman Catholic priest

• 17-year-old female; White; waitress; high school dropout; supports/cares for a brother who is severely disabled

• 38-year-old female, White, AIDS researcher, no children, lesbian

Refrain from giving any further instructions or suggestions. Allow at least 20 minutes for decision making. Then reconvene the class and question each group about its decision and its decision-making process. Facilitate discussion.

Discussion Questions:
1. What was your decision?
2. How did you arrive at your decision.
3. What decision-making method did you use (consensus, voting, etc.)?
4. How was your decision influenced by your values? ...your attitudes? ...your prejudices?
5. Who provided leadership in your group?
6. How were disagreements and conflicts handled?
7. How satisfied are you with your own level of participation in this exercise?

Motivation

Young people who have developed positive attitudes, who have transformed their dreams into goals, who work at liking and respecting themselves, and who have learned to make sound decisions and solve simple and complex problems, need only one more thing to reach their dreams — resilient, renewable motivation.

What keeps successful people going? What skills, attributes, and values distinguish people who achieve their dreams from those who do not. The activities in this unit give students several opportunities to answer these questions. Through inquiry, interviews, and research, students attempt to unravel the secrets of successful people. In addition, they examine sources of influence in their own lives, and evaluate their use (and misuse) of their most precious resource — time.

Significant People Who Have Influenced My Life
Creative Writing and Discussion

Objectives:
The students will:
—describe people who have influenced them.
—compare the process of influence with the process of leadership.

Materials:
writing materials for the students

Directions:
Begin by discussing with the class how people can strongly affect other people's lives. Point out that individuals whom we admire and respect become models. They become our mentors in life.

Explain the writing assignment. Tell the students that they are to think and write about people who have significantly shaped their lives. Ask them to describe how each individual affected them, acknowledging that in some cases the impact may have been negative or mixed. Allow ample time for writing.

Have the students share their writings in dyads, triads, or small groups. Ask them to omit the names and relationships of people who affected them negatively. Facilitate a culminating class discussion.

Discussion Questions:
1. What characteristics or qualities did the people who influenced us seem to share?
2. How much of who you are today was influenced by other people?
3. For someone to influence you, don't you have to (in a sense) give your permission? Explain.
4. Whose lives might *you* be influencing, and how?

How They Got Where They Are Today

Interviews, Reports, and Class Discussion

Objectives:

The students will:

—describe characteristics of successful people.

—learn and practice specific interviewing techniques.

Materials:

one copy of the interview form for each student; writing materials; optional student-obtained tape recorders for interviews; chart paper and markers

Directions:

Begin this activity by asking the students what they think are the main characteristics of successful people. Facilitate discussion and write suggestions on chart paper so that the list can be saved.

Ask the students to think of people *they know* who are successful in their profes-

sions or active in community organizations. Ask them to each choose one person—a relative, friend, or acquaintance—with whom they will be able to arrange an interview.

Distribute the interview forms. Go over the questions provided, and urge the students to think of additional questions that they would like to ask the person they interview. Spend some time talking about interview skills. Generate a list of guidelines on the board, including:

• Explain the purpose of the interview: to gain information about successful living from people whom they admire and respect.

• Establish the length of the interview in advance; for example, 15 to 30 minutes. Stick to that agreement, beginning and ending on time.

• Ask each question clearly, and then listen carefully to the answer, jotting down abbreviated notes. Fill in the details immediately after the interview.

• As much as possible, maintain eye contact.

• If you don't understand something, ask for clarification. For example, say, "I'm not sure I understand," or "Would you please say more about that?" or "Can you give me an example?"

• Paraphrase and feed back some of the interviewee's answers to ensure understanding. For example, begin with, "What I hear you saying is that..." or "It sounds like you mean..."

• Keep the focus on the interviewee and avoid interrupting.

• Thank the interviewee upon concluding the interview.

Explain that the information gained from the interview may be presented either orally or in writing. For students who choose to deliver their reports orally, allow 3 to 5 minutes per report. As the reports are made, ask the "audience" to list any and all special qualities identified through the interviews. After all of the reports have been given, compile a list of qualities on the board. Tape up the original list beside the new one and compare. Facilitate discussion.

Discussion Questions:

1. How did the people we interviewed become successful?
2. What did most of the people we interviewed seem to have in common?
3. What were the five most frequently mentioned qualities?
4. Were any of the qualities stressed by the interviewees absent from our first list? What were they?
5. Did we have anything on our first list that they didn't think was important?
6. What are some characteristics and behaviors these people did *not* have?
7. How do you think these people measure their success, other than through money, possessions, and an influential position?

Interview Form

Interview a successful person. You may interview someone who is a supervisor in a large organization, a leader in the community, a person who is very creative, like an artist or musician, an athlete who is highly skilled in his or her event or sport, or someone who has become wealthy through wise investements — anyone you think leads an exemplary life. Use these questions and develop three of your own.

1. What is your title or position? _____

_____

2. What are your main responsibilities in the position? _____

_____

_____

3. How much of your job involves leadership? _____

_____

_____

4. What do you think has made you successful? _____

_____

_____

5. What principles or values do you live by? _____

_____

_____

_____

6. What personal qualities do you think are required to be successful?

_____

_____

_____

_____

7. What suggestions do you have for young people who want to succeed?

_____

_____

_____

_____

8. _____

_____

_____

_____

9. _____

_____

_____

_____

10. _____

_____

_____

_____

Managing Time
Discussion and Experience Sheet

Objectives:

The students will:
—evaluate their use of time.
—identify time-wasters and ways to reduce or eliminate them.
—explain the relationship between time management and goal attainment.

Materials:

one copy of the experience sheet, "Control Your Time," for each student; chalkboard and chalk or chart paper and markers

Directions:

Begin be reminding the students of the importance of goals. After reviewing some of the concepts they have discussed concerning setting and attaining goals, point out that one of the hardest things about attaining goals—particularly long-range goals—is making the time to do what's needed to reach them.

In your own words, explain: *Most of us are pretty good at reaching short-term goals. We do it every day. One reason is that short-term goals usually have short-term deadlines. For example, if you don't make that phone call this afternoon, you won't know if your plans for tomorrow are on or off. If you don't finish your homework early, you won't be able to watch TV. If you don't repair your bike before the weekend, the Saturday morning ride is off.*

Long-range goals often don't have deadlines at all. At least not at first. Instead, they require careful planning and the completion of lots of small tasks. Going to Europe after graduation, for example, involves earning and saving money, making travel arrangements, getting a passport, deciding where to go, what to see, how to travel, where to stay, and whom to go with, just for starters. A long-range goal without a plan is just a dream.

Try to get in the habit of writing down all the steps required to reach a goal. Then start taking those steps right away. Even if your goal is five years down the road, there are things that you can do about it now! Getting control of your time will allow you to take daily, weekly, or monthly steps toward your long-range goals.

Distribute the experience sheets. Give the students a few minutes to complete the sheet. Then have them form small groups and share their "day pies," and identified time-wasters. Suggest that the groups generate additional ideas for controlling and eliminating time-wasters. Conclude the activity with a class discussion.

Discussion Questions:

1. What did your "day pie" tell you about the time you spend doing various things?
2. What changes would you like to make in your use of time?
3. What were the biggest time-wasters in your group?
4. Which ideas for reducing or eliminating time-wasters are most likely to work for you?
5. What have been the biggest time-wasters in organizations and groups to which you've belonged?

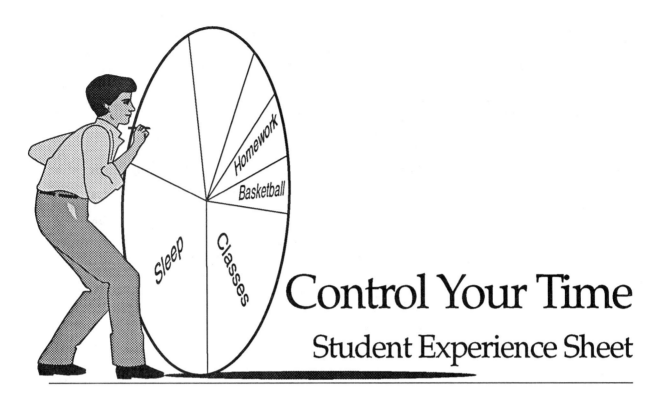

Control Your Time
Student Experience Sheet

Make a "Day Pie."

Estimate how many hours or parts of hours you spend in school, sleeping, doing homework, earning money, eating, watching TV, playing, reading, working, and other things. Label each piece of your "day pie" to show the major activity it represents. Once you've completed the pie, take a good look at it.

Are you satisfied with how you spend your time?

Where can you fit in the steps you must take to reach your long-range goals?

Control time-wasters.

It has been said that, "You waste your time whenever you spend it doing something less important when you could be doing something more important." Do you agree with that statement? Why or why not?

To determine whether or not an activity is a time-waster for you, measure it against your goals. Is the activity helping you reach your goals? If not, how can you reduce or eliminate the time you devote to it?

Put a ✔ beside your time-wasters.

___**Telephone.** If you are frequently interrupted by phone calls while studying or working on an important project, try asking your friends to call you at an agreed-upon hour. Set aside a special time each day to make outgoing calls, too. Limit each call to a few minutes.

___**Television.** It's okay to watch your favorite shows, but don't watch TV just to fill (or kill) time. Instead, use that time to do something that will move you in the direction of a goal!

__Cluttered room, work area, or desk.__ How much time do you waste looking for misplaced items? Not very many people can do their best work amid disorganization. Take some time to "shape up" your space. Have at hand all necessary tools and materials. For studying, you'll need such things as books, paper, pens, pencils, calculator, notebooks, notes, erasers, dictionary, software, and any assistive devices you use.

__Socializing.__ Being with friends is important, but try not to let socializing distract you from other things that you've decided to do. When you plan your day, allow ample time for enjoyable interaction with friends and family. Then, when it's time to work on other goals, don't socialize.

__Poor communication.__ If you frequently fail to understand your assignments, misinterpret statements made by friends or family, or have trouble getting your own ideas across, put some extra effort into communicating effectively. Over 90 percent of all communication is oral (spoken). That means you need to 1) state your own thoughts accurately and clearly, and 2) listen actively and attentively. Phrase your ideas in two or three different ways until you are certain others understand them. When listening, paraphrase what you've heard (restate it in your own words) or ask questions to ensure understanding.

__Lack of planning.__ Always write down your goals, assignments, appointments, chores, and job schedule. Then work out a weekly plan and follow it. With a plan, you'll never have to waste time wondering what to do next.

__Poor study habits.__ Here are some tips: Study at a desk or table. List your assignments in the order in which you plan to do them. Complete your most difficult assignments first while you are alert. Study without interruptions (phone calls) and distractions (TV or radio). Take frequent short breaks. As you read, write down questions that cross your mind. Ask those questions in class or discuss them with a friend. Periodically study with a classmate. Complete reading assignments before they are discussed in class.

__Procrastination.__ Most of us tend to put off things that are unpleasant, things that are difficult, and things that involve tough decisions. These are often the very things that contribute most to our success! Try these procrastination cures:

• Do unpleasant tasks first. Or do them in small pieces, setting a deadline for each.

• Break down difficult tasks into smaller parts. Keep breaking down the parts until you see the first step.

• Break down difficult tasks into "minijobs." Make each minijob small enough to finish in less than 10 minutes.

• Get more information. A task may seem difficult simply because you don't know enough about it. The more you know, the more likely you are to become interested and involved.

How I Influence Others
Creative Writing and Discussion

Objectives:

The students will;

—define influence and describe how people influence one another.

—describe one or more ways in which they influence others.

Materials:

writing materials; art supplies (optional)

Directions:

Introduce the activity by talking with the students about the concept of *influence*. Ask the students to help you brainstorm ideas related to influence. Facilitate a wide-ranging exploration of the concept. Write key terms and phrases on the chalkboard. Here are some possibilities:

• Influence is often subtle.

• Influence is a form of power.

• The ability to influence is one of the main qualities that defines successful people.

• People who are popular and/or admired have influence.

• Sources of influence include peers, parents, teachers, role models, idols, and advertising

• Groups and crowds influence by sheer numbers.

• People are influenced both consciously and unconsciously.

• Influence often occurs by example.

• Many people aren't aware of how much influence they have.

• Most decisions are based on an interplay of influences.

Tell the students that you'd like them to explore some of the ways they influence other people. Explain that they can fulfill the assignment by writing a story, poem, essay, or short play, or by creating a cartoon. Suggest that they use one of the topics provided, or develop their own.

List the following topics on the board:

Ways I've Influenced Others
How I Got Someone to Change an
Opinion
Everybody Started Feeling the Same
Way I Was Feeling
How I Got a Person to Stop Doing
Something
I Put Pressure on Someone
I Set an Example for Someone Younger
Than Me

Allow ample time for the students to work on the assignment. Follow your preferred editing/rewriting procedure.

Invite volunteers to share their finished stories with the class. Identify the types, qualities, and targets of influence in each example and discuss the results. When the sharing is complete facilitate a summary discussion.

Discussion Questions:
1. What have you learned about influence from this assignment?
2. What have you learned about *your* ability to influence?
3. What determines whether or not you can influence someone?
4. How does knowing about influence help you accept or resist it in someone else?

Measuring Success

Experience Sheet and Discussion

Objectives:
The students will
—identify specific ways in which they limit themselves.
—describe how self-limitations are formed and ways they can be eliminated.

Materials:
one copy of the experience sheet, "Success Takes Guts," for each student

Directions:
Ask the students to turn to the experience sheet, "Success Takes Guts." Give them a couple of minutes to read the story, "The Jar of Fleas." Elicit the reactions of the students, helping them view the story is analogous to situations in which people fail because they don't expect to succeed in the first place. Point out that there are, from time to time, *real* lids on our lives that keep us from doing things we could otherwise do, just as there really was a lid on the jar of fleas *for awhile.* However, things change, and all too often we think there are lids above us that aren't there anymore.

Ask the students to think of ways in which they limit themselves. Write some of their suggestions on the board.

Give the students time to complete the experience sheet. Have them share their responses in dyads. Lead a culminating discussion.

Discussion Questions:
1. Can you think of a mistake you've made only once? What was it?
2. Why do we fear criticism?
3. How can we develop an ability to listen to criticism without feeling so bad?
4. Why do some of us remember our mistakes and failures better than we remember our successes? How can we reverse that tendency?

Success Takes Guts
Student Experience Sheet

The Jar of Fleas

Old Harry Fretchit wanted to train some new fleas for his flea circus, so he hung out with some cats and dogs until he caught about ten nice, strong, high-jumping fleas. Harry wanted fleas that were strong and healthy, so the higher they jumped, the better. But you can't train a flea who can jump clear across the room without first getting its attention.

So high jumping was the first habit of Harry's new fleas that he had to break. How he did it was very interesting.

At first, the fleas were in a big cage where they had plenty of jumping room. So Harry patiently transferred them to a jar about five inches high. After that, each time a flea jumped, he banged his whole body on the lid of the jar. Obviously, continual body banging felt very uncomfortable to the fleas. As a result, they began to jump with less vigor, so

that when they banged themselves it wouldn't hurt so bad (but it still hurt). After a while, they jumped with even *less* vigor, until finally one flea made a very weak jump and went down again without banging himself at all! As soon as the other fleas saw this, they copied him, and pretty soon all of the fleas were jumping up and down inside the jar without hitting the lid.

Harry had been watching, but he didn't take the lid off—yet. He wanted the fleas to get so used to having the lid there, and jumping little jumps, that they wouldn't miss the lid after it was gone. They would not even *remember* how to make big jumps.

And that's exactly what happened. After several more days, Harry took off the lid and, sure enough, there were those poor little fleas jumping up and down, but never higher than four-and-three-quarters inches for the rest of their lives.

Take a look. Are there any imaginary lids above you?

Write down some of the ways you limit yourself.

1. _____

2. _____

3. _____

Sometimes people stop themselves from doing things. Later, they ask themselves, "Why didn't I do that?"

Describe a time when you stopped yourself from doing something that you really wanted to do.

_____

_____

_____

What stopped you? _____

_____

_____

Just in case, like the fleas, you've forgotten some of *your* capabilities, take the time to remember them now. Complete the following:

SomethingI did during the first five years of my life that was successful:

_____

During the time I was in elementary school, I succeeded at: _____

_____

When I was in junior high school, one of my successes was:_____

_____

Since I've been in high school, I've succeeded at:_____

_____

Something I can show other people how to do is: _____

I am admired by someone for my ability to:_____

A game I usually win is: _____

The subject I'm best at in school is:_____

I feel very proud of myself when I: _____

A job or duty I'm good at is: _____

A positive habit I've got that I'm pleased with is: _____

Six things I like about myself are:

1._____   4._____

2._____   5._____

3._____   6._____

Some people limit themselves because they fear criticism. Other people fear failure. Quite a few fear both. If you fit any of these categories, remember to:

    1. See and believe in each one of your achievements.
    2. Exercise your right to accept or reject criticism based on its worth and value to you.
    3. Accept failure as an occasional price of trying.

These People Did

Research, Creative Writing, and Role Plays

Objectives:

The students will:
— research the lives of people who have contributed significantly to the betterment of the world.
— describe how people contribute through organized action.

Materials:

biographies; simple props for the role plays (optional)

Directions:

Discuss with the students how the world has often been made better by what a single individual has chosen to do, frequently against strong opposition or general apathy.

Tell the students that during the next week (or two), their assignment will be to read books or articles about such a person, and then write a short dramatic scene or sequence about a significant incident in that person's life—a moment when that *one* individual made a difference.

The following individuals are all 19th or 20th century American reformers, easily researchable, and by almost anyone's standards, altruistic and idealistic.

Robert Owen
Lucy Stone
John Peter Altgeld
Susan B. Anthony
Julia Ward Howe
Frederick Douglas
Dorothea Dix
Elizabeth Cady Stanton
Amos Bronson Alcott
William Lloyd Garrison
Harriet Tubman
Dag Hammerskjold
Clara Barton

Ralph Nader
Anthony Comstock
Samuel Gridley Howe
John Muir
Jane Addams
Martin Luther King
Sojourner Truth
John Humphrey Noyes

Add names of your own to this list and urge the students to do likewise. (There are many excellent reference books with short biographies of people who changed the world for the better.) Also list organizations such as the United Nations, UNICEF, the Sierra Club, and other public interest groups that work to effect social and political changes that benefit large numbers of people.

Have the students work in groups of two to six to conduct their research. When the groups have been established, ask them to select one student to act as coordinator. Suggest that individual assignments be planned to avoid duplication of effort, and a reasonable amount of time allowed for research and reading.

In a later session, have each group meet separately to plan and rehearse a 3- to 4-minute dramatic scene illustrating a key incident in the life of the person researched. The presentations should include a short introduction that tells the other students something about the person whose life is being dramatized, what the person accomplished during his or her lifetime, etc. Allow one or two sessions for the presentations. After each presentation, lead a discussion.

Discussion Questions:

1. What motivated this person (or organization) to take action?
2. What were some of the obstacles encountered?
3. How were the obstacles overcome?
4. Did the person (or organization), during his/her own life, feel that he or she had accomplished something that had really changed conditions in the world?
5. What have you learned about community action from this activity?

More Products from INNERCHOICE PUBLISHING

New products are routinely added to our collection of books and materials for counselors and teachers. Here are a few samples. For a FREE CATALOG, call, write, or fax Innerchoice Publishing, P.O. Box 2476, Spring Valley, CA 91979 (619) 698-2437   698-3348 (Fax)

IMPACT!
A Self-Esteem Based Skill Development Program for Secondary Students

This exceptional program-in-a-kit facilitates the growth of secondary students in the social and emotional domains by teaching skills that are essential to self-esteem. *IMPACT!* is an ideal tool for counselors, and may be integrated by teachers into virtually any subject area, infusing the regular curriculum with life skills and personal relevancy. *IMPACT!* increases the ability of students to function effectively in a multicultural environment, and encourages them to recognize their broader role as members of society. The kit also includes a poster and a companion text containing Circle Session discussion topics and guidelines.

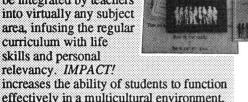

COUNSELOR IN THE CLASSROOM
Activities and Strategies for an Effective Classroom Guidance Program

This up-to-the-minute approach to school counseling is packed with instantly usable activities to help you increase your value as a counselor by working cooperatively with teachers to provide guidance activities and instruction — right in the classroom. Each activity is a 30-40 minute lesson, and many include reproducibles to leave with the teacher. Just a few of the theme areas are Understanding Feelings, Handling Peer Pressure, Developing Classroom Rules; Self-Management Skills; Being Home Alone; Creative/ Critical Thinking; Developing Positive Attitudes, and Dealing with Crises and Loss.

UNDERSTANDING ME
Activity Sheets for Building Life Skills and Self-Esteem in Secondary Students

Over 85 pages of reproducible activity sheets! Use them to enhance the self-esteem of teenagers while developing critical life skills. Topics addressed include Decision Making, Goal Setting, Communication, Feelings, Trust, Helping, Being a Teenager, Culture, Friendship, and Winning and Losing.

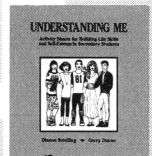

ACTIVITIES FOR COUNSELING UNDERACHIEVERS

This is a new companion book to Jeanne C. Bleuer's *Counseling Under-achievers*, which you will also find in our catalog. It contains surveys and assessments that help students identify perceptions that contribute to under-achievement, and lots of helpful activities in areas like Getting along with others; Asking for and getting help; Being comfortable in school; Study skills; Self-esteem and personal strengths.

TEACHING THE SKILLS OF CONFLICT RESOLUTION
Activities and Strategies for Counseling and Teaching

This thoroughly useful activity book will help you reduce classroom and school conflicts through the creation of a more peaceful, cooperative learning environ-ment, and give students tools to resolve and learn from conflicts when they occur. Activities help students deal with their feelings; appreciate and include others; practice effective communication, problem-solving and decision-making; reduce stress, and learn specific conflict resolution and peer-mediation skills.

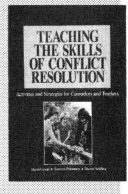

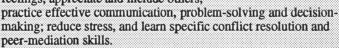